20 WAYS TO TRACK A TIGER

EXPLORING WITH
FILMMAKER • PHOTOGRAPHER
CAROL AMORE

WildlifeWorlds

Dedicated to wild tigers, tiger trackers, elephant mahavats and their Asian elephants, forest guides, tiger researchers, conservationists, and concerned individuals who work to save tigers and made this book possible.

A special dedication to my mother and father for their entrepreneurial encouragement.

May these wild tiger photographs inspire new ways to keep tigers free and people their protectors.

Purchase books and DVDs for schools, corporate events/gifts, and friends of wild tigers at www.wildlifeworlds.com

Library of Congress Control Number: 2003091846

ISBN 1-930419066

Editor: Sharon AvRutick
Designer: Daisuke Endo
Mapmakers: Connie Brown and Julie Ruff, Redstone Studios
Web Designer: Isabel Chang

Printer: Finlay Printing, Bloomfield, Connecticut

Publisher: Wildlife Worlds—Adventures in Nature Productions

A portion of the proceeds from the sale of this book will be donated to saving tigers.

WildlifeWorlds

Left: A hairy eyelid protects the delicate and ever-watchful eye of the tigertracking Asian elephant from dust.

Previous pages: The Bandhavgarh Fort Hill (right) and Bandhini Hill (left) dominate the view from Rajbehra Waterhole in the Bandhavgarh Tiger Reserve.

CONTENTS

The tower-like interlocking vines and branches of India's sacred banyan tree, several hundred years old, create an umbrella of shade, granting tigers and other wildlife relief from the intense sun.

THE SPIRIT OF AN EXPLORER

Imagine yourself on top of an elephant tracking a Bengal tiger through the Indian jungle, surrounded by a breathtaking array of wildlife and vegetation. You are deep in carnivore country surrounded by unfamiliar animal sounds. The elephant trumpets to signal the location of a tiger. You are fascinated and perhaps more than a little frightened, but you are spurred on by your limitless curiosity and the desire to find a tiger. You are an explorer.

You follow the direction of local forest guards and elephant guides (mahavats), who know all the nuances of finding tigers in every season. You remain alert to every detail of your environment, from the dirt trail to the skies above, whether it's a paw print, claw marks in trees, or the calls of carnivorous birds. In the rare moments when all these clues and the guides' expertise converge, finding an endangered tiger becomes a reality.

During my nonstop three-month film expedition to India's Bandhavgarh Tiger Reserve, my team and I endured an assortment of physical challenges—the intense summer heat (110° F/43° C), whip-like bamboo branches, malaria-infested forests—while protecting the camera equipment from damage and living with the constant pressures—and dangers—involved in photographing and filming tigers every day. Throughout, the spirit of the filming was to capture images and sounds of a tiger family at those rare times when they would tolerate our presence while at the same time respecting their world. We were successful, going home with over 150 hours of wild Bengal tiger footage to help tell a most compelling story and make the film *Tigers—Tracking a Legend*.

The photographs in this volume were made on the back of an elephant or on top of a 10-foot (3.05 m) tripod within close range of the tigers, the vantage point from which I shot the film. My use of the latest high-definition video technology enabled me to create images with remarkable sharpness and clarity. All the details of the tiger's body, face, whiskers, and even the tip of its tail are there; you can practically reach out and touch the tiger.

But my high-tech tools were only one part of the equation. To tell the world about what we had the privilege to witness, we drew on a reserve of all the skills and abilities an explorer must have. We kept a clear focus on our goals, trusted intuition, dealt with chaos under pressure, took appropriate risks, tapped inner reserves of stamina, managed fears with insight, endured physical hardships, focused on the positive, and found time to laugh at the toughest challenges.

Explorers engineer their own destiny. My destiny is finding and helping to save tigers, the most awesome and alluring of all big cats. As you track the tigers in this photography book, my hope is that you will find the inspiration and impetus to join me in helping these wild tigers and their habitats in Asia, and to engineer your own destiny as an explorer.

In the Bandhavgarh Tiger Reserve, tiger dancers—devotees to Durga, the Hindu goddess who rides a tiger or lion and is both benign and a powerful demon slayer—spin to the riveting rhythm of beating drums. With their painted striped bodies, the dancers swirl and enter into a ritual dream state, hoping for Durga's good favor. Dancers grasp symbolic dagger-like claws to evoke the spirit of the tiger in each person, giving them strength, speed, and power. They carry forward the affinity and fascination humans have with tigers and all they represent throughout the world.

BANDHAVGARH TIGER RESERVE

For centuries, India's maharajas tracked tigers on their royal hunting grounds, believing they would earn good luck by killing 109 trophy tigers. At the same time, they helped conserve the forest and its wildlife. Many of their lands are now tiger reserves. The Bandhavgarh Tiger Reserve is a case in point: From the twelfth to the early seventeenth century, the family of the Maharaja of Rewa lived and hunted in its forests, but in 1968, as the tiger's numbers declined through hunting and poaching, the property became a preserve intended to help protect the tiger and its habitat.

Thirty or forty Bengal tigers live in the 173 square miles (450 sq km) of the Bandhavgarh Tiger Reserve, located in the Vindhya hills of India's Madhya Pradesh. (*Bandhav* means "brother" and *garh* means "fort"; the name derives from the idea that Lord Rama supposedly gave the 2000-year-old fort on the site to his brother Laksmana.) The rich variety of geographic features within the reserve—hills with many caves; low-lying areas with about twenty spring-fed streams; grasslands, bamboo thickets, marshy areas, open stream banks, and waterholes—attracts some thirty-five species of large and small mammals, including a dense deer population. Some 242 bird species enjoy the full range of ecosystems within the reserve, including the magnificent Malabar hornbills flying above the fort. Dominating the landscape of the park are the Bandhavgarh Plateau and Bandhini Hill, rising to 2,625 feet (800 m) above sea level. These cliffs are ideal nesting sites for such raptors as white-backed vultures and crested serpent eagles.

Bandhavgarh's moist, tropical forests are at least 80 percent sal trees (*Shorea robusta*), and there is plentiful bamboo (*Dendrocalamus strictus*). Average annual rainfall is 50 inches (1.2 m), most of which falls during the monsoon (mid-June through September), and during the winter.

Bandhavgarh's Tigers: Familiar Territories, 1999–2000

Bachhi spent most of her time in the Bandhini Hill cave area. It has lots of ledges that are easy for the cubs to climb and that provide good lookouts, and there's a small spring-fed water hole a short distance away. It was extremely difficult to track Bachhi and her cubs by elephant in this region.

Bhadrashila Caves have a large nearby waterhole with rich meadow grasses and plenty of grazing chital nearby. Bachhi is believed to have been born here.

The Thaudi Caves are on a sloping elevated ridge overlooking a wide waterhole and plentiful meadow grasses. Tigers prefer the nearby Akela Kunda Waterhole, which offers shade from the sun through the day.

The Chorbehra Cave area has several sandy ravines (*nallas*) leading to a labyrinth of rocks and ledges featuring lots of escape routes for cubs to follow to escape from approaching predators.

The former dominant male, Charger, had only a small territory mostly from the Chorbehra area to Bandhini Hill.

Banda, the ascendant male, especially liked one Rajbehra cave with its cool, long corridor entrance and its nearby expansive meadows for hunting.

Left: The Maharaja of Rewa's ancestors used this gun to hunt tigers on the land that is now a tiger reserve.

Map: Connie Brown, Redstone Studios

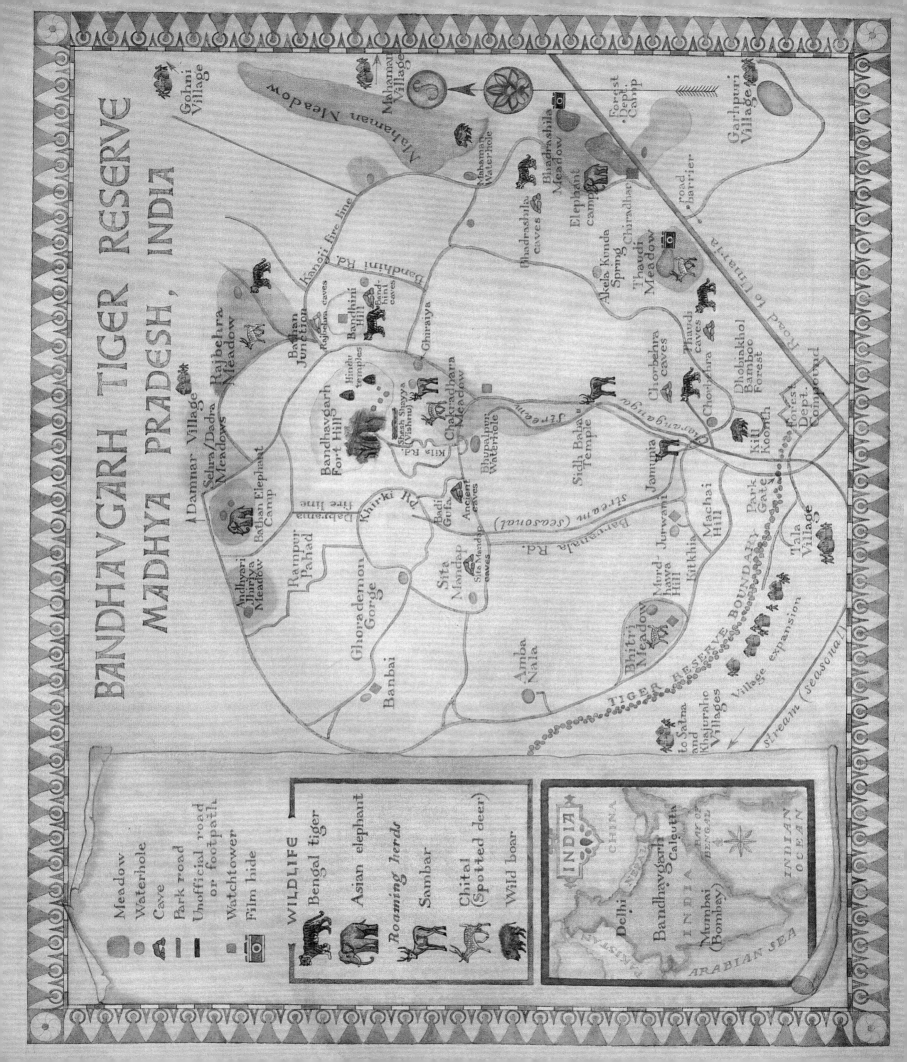

TRACKING A LEGEND: MEET THE FAMILY

Filmed in India's Bandhavgarh Tiger Reserve, the documentary *Tigers—Tracking a Legend* traces the lives of a wild Bengal tigress, Bachhi, and her two young cubs, Badi and Choti. As they grow, the cubs face a variety of threats from cobras and pythons to sloth bears, leopards, and even other tigers. In the surrounding forest, another drama unfolds: Charger, an old dominant male tiger, is being challenged by his son Banda.

Tracking a Legend

The cast of characters from the film make a series of cameo appearances throughout these pages as they were tracked through the jungle. Follow your favorite tigers and learn about their lives.

Follow "Tracking a Legend" story clues. As you read this book, be alert for insights into the daily drama of the relationships between these Bandhavgarh tigers, which can be witnessed in the *Tigers—Tracking a Legend* film.

BANDA, whose name means "crooked tail," is the son of Bachhi from her first litter in 1997 and is now the ascendant male of Bandhavgarh. Three years old, he is a masterful hunter, at the top of his game. But like any adult male, he poses a real threat to Bachhi's young cubs. Killing them would bring Bachhi into estrus sooner and give Banda a chance to produce his own cubs. He does successfully mate with a tigress named Sita-Wali.

BACHHI whose name means "young girl" in Hindi, is six years old and is raising her second litter. She gave birth to her daughters Choti and Badi in October 1999. Bachhi, a most successful hunter with a trim physique, weighs about 300 pounds (135 kg), about eight times the weight of a cub at the age of five months.

CHOTI, whose name, a term of endearment, means "small," is timid and affectionate, clinging to her mother whenever she can. She has heart-shaped stripes covering her right elbow. She needs more encouragement to feel at ease in coming out of the cave and in being assertive with her bigger sister.

CHARGER is a seventeen-year-old male born in 1990 who dominated the Bandhavgarh Tiger Reserve territory for most of a decade. He earned his name by charging jeeps with ferocious growls. But now, past his prime, he's being challenged by a younger, stronger male, his son Banda. Charger's senses have declined and he has to steal food to survive. Most wild tigers live about twelve to fifteen years. During his long reign, Charger sired at least seven litters and seventeen tigers, including Choti and Badi as well as their mother, Bachhi. Such inbreeding is not unusual in a small tiger population like that of Bandhavgarh.

BADI, or "big," is larger and more aggressive than her sister. She always tries to get the spot right next to her mother at mealtime (this is where the most food is available), and she frequently wins wrestling matches with Choti. She is destined to grow up to be a great hunter.

Right: Bachhi, the tigress, with her two energetic and fast-growing female cubs Choti (being pounced on) and Badi at Bandhini Hill Waterhole.

1

PARTNER WITH ELEPHANT MAHAVATS

The best way to see a Bengal tiger is to work with a mahavat, or mahout, a dedicated forest guide and master of the art of tiger tracking. He does his job on the back of his Asian elephant partner who safely maneuvers him through dense woods and bamboo forests. At first light and again at dusk, the mahavats accurately read the tiger tracks on loose dirt roads, riverbanks, dry riverbeds, and around waterholes, where existing tiger territories are known. Staying in contact with each other with field radios, by calling with high-pitched hoots, and by having their elephants trumpet when they find a tiger, mahavats exchange updated information about the movements of the tigers and their prey. The tiger-tracking season is usually from November through June. The monsoon rains hinder travel through the jungle from mid-June through September.

Perched on a saddle (*howdah*) which can weigh 70 pounds (32 kg) or more, mahavats routinely deal with an array of physical challenges—whether it's being hit by swinging bamboo branches, having their legs crushed between the elephant and a tree, or removing a poisonous snake or biting red ants that have dropped on them from above. Sometimes when the difficulties become too many, the tiger-tracking team may ceremoniously offer a *puja*, or prayer, to the elephant-headed Hindu god Ganesha, remover of obstacles.

The mahavats and their elephants—which are never truly domesticated—protect the tigers from poachers in the reserve. Mahavats also look for signs of distress in the tigers, such as excessive panting (which can indicate infection), thinning fur and scabs (signs of parasites, fleas, and ticks), and excessive aggressiveness (which can be due to physical injury). Avoid injured tigers. They can attack unpredictably.

Dodging low-lying limbs, the elephant and mahavat, guardians of the tigers in the reserve, maneuver like an agile chariot through the dense forest obstacle course from dawn through dusk, with a midday break.

Mahavats communicate intuitively with their elephants, each of which has a unique personality, by using a synchronized combination of spoken Hindi and barefoot commands. Elephants' low-frequency sounds travel for miles through the thick forest and hilly terrain, allowing them to hear each other as well as the sounds of tigers.

1

 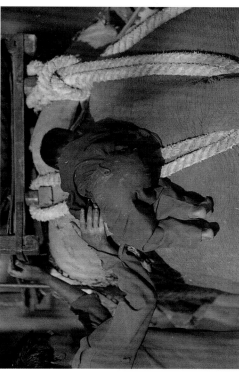 

The mahavat Dayaram saddles Wanraj with a *howdah*, getting ready to go tiger tracking out of Bhadrashila Elephant Camp. Lalu gains traction from the elephant's rough-textured skin and uses a boost from his father and the thick saddle ropes to pull himself up on the elephant.

Talking to the Mahavat

Hello: *Namaste*
Please: *Kri-paa ho-gee*
Thanks: *Dhanyavaad*
Yes: *Jee-haan*
No: *Jee na-heen*
Okay: *Theek-hai*

Bengal tiger: *Bagh, Sher*
Tiger cub: *Bagh ka-bacha*
Asian elephant: *Hathi* (male), *Hathni* (female)
Sloth bear: *bhalu*
Indian leopard: *Tendwa*
Cobra: *Naag*
Python: *ajgar*

Straight ahead: *See dhaa aage*
How far?: *Kit-nee door*
Right: *Daa-en-ta-raf*
Left: *Baa-en-ta-raf*

Listen: *Su-ni-ye*
Lookout!: *De-khi-ye*
Danger: *Khat-raa*
Help!: *Ba-chaa-o!*

Mahavats' Elephant Commands

The mahavat has a strong bond with the elephant built over many years. A combination of verbal and foot commands made behind the elephant's ear or on top of its head usually signal the speed and direction in which to travel.

Go forward: *Mal*
Stop: *Dhat*
Back up: *Piche*
Turn: *Chi ghun*
Lift: *Uthao*
Sit down: *Sum baith*
Lie down on belly: *Tire*
Lie down on side: *Dhar uthao*

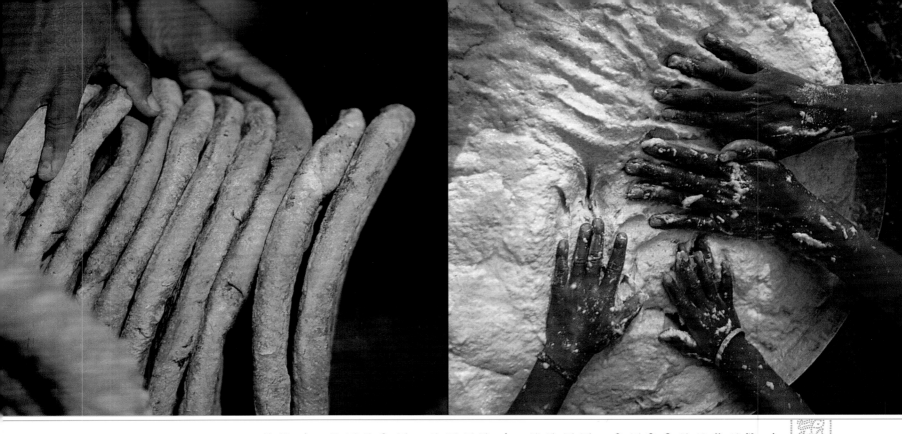

The mahavats have to care for their elephants, giving the gentle giants daily baths to remove parasites and checking their toes; elephants walk exclusively on their toes, and if they are injured, they cannot track. Mahavats also must ensure that the elephants have enough to eat. Elephants need to eat a tremendous amount, about 450 pounds (200 kg) of green foliage every day; they forage constantly. Since the tracking elephants don't have a chance to forage while they're out on patrol, mahavats supplement their wild food with elephant-sized rations of high-energy chapati bread.

Elephants sleep for only about four to six hours at night, lying down for a mere two hours at a time. They spend the rest of the night on their feet, eating and sleeping, and sleep intermittently during the day, again on their feet.

The most challenging and life-threatening moment for a mahavat is when his bull elephant enters musth, a period of heightened aggression often associated with breeding, which happens once a year or more often. The first indication of musth is a secretion at the elephant's temple.

Like the tiger, the Asian elephant (*Elephas maximus*) is endangered, with fewer than 40,000 remaining in the wild. The unique relationship they have with the mahavats helps protect both wild species and preserves a centuries-old way of life for the men. Mahavats exist in only a few select sites in India.

The mahavat, elephant, and tiger have a strange and wonderful partnership in reserves—one upon which their mutual survival depends. And tiger tracking is the key to it all.

1

Left: Dayaram and Lalu make chapati breads, a snack for their trusted tiger-tracking elephant, Wanraj. Their hands pump in a hypnotic rhythm as they knead the sticky dough. When the huge, flat round breads are ready, they place them directly into the droopy pink mouths of the elephants, who jostle each other in excitement.

Right: Little Lalu, seven years old, washes three-ton Wanraj. After splashing him with water, Lalu selects a stone of just the right texture, and begins to scour the wrinkled gray skin, paying particular attention to the area around the eye. One wrong move and Lalu could be crushed, since the elephant is about 150 times bigger than he is.

Tracking a Legend

Bachhi, the tigress, and her two spirited female cubs can often be found at the waterhole at the beginning and end of the day, quenching their thirst in the intense (110° F/43° C) summer heat. While the mahavat and his son wait at the Bathan Waterhole, hopeful that the family will arrive for a vital afternoon drink, they enjoy watching the naturally playful wild Asian elephants sloshing through the water and slinging mud into the air.

Above: Dayaram, the elephant mahavat, and his son Lalu offer a *puja* (prayer) to the Hindu god Ganesha, remover of obstacles, asking for good fortune in finding the tigers.

Right: Even though tigers might drink nearby, young wild Asian elephants delight in wrestling, splashing with their powerful, rubbery trunks, and diving underwater in the cool waterhole in the midday sun. Afterward, they take an entertaining dust bath, using the dirt like a sunscreen. The Asian elephant's trunk has 40,000 muscles with one flexible finger at its end, capable of delicate maneuvers like peeling bark off trees and picking up sticks, stones, and even film cartridges.

1

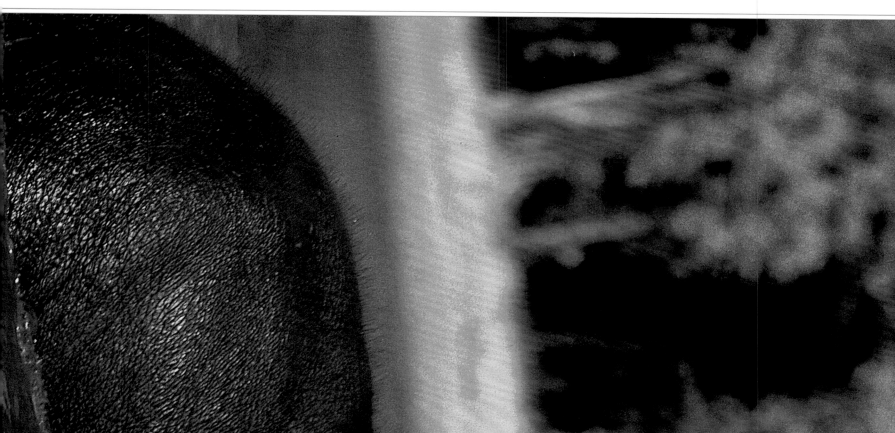

1

Left: Camouflaged in the bamboo, Bachhi watches attentively as the elephant approaches. Depending on its level of familiarity with elephants, each tiger has its own comfort zone —about 30–60 feet (9–18 m)—that it will allow before it reacts to the intrusion. Sometimes, the tiger may be calm, and other times it may show its annoyance with a hiss, growl, or rapidly flicking tail.

Right, top: Banda, the ascendant male tiger, rests calmly in the cool shade at the waterhole during the heat of the day, while the elephant takes in some of its daily 40–50 gallons (150–190 l) of water.

Right, bottom: The elephant sometimes trumpets on the mahavat's command to signal to other mahavats in the jungle that the tiger is found.

How do tigers and elephants get along?

The tigers in Bandhavgarh Tiger Reserve are habituated to the mahavats' elephants and generally accept their close presence, particularly when they see them tracking every day. Some young tigers even run to the elephants for protection, especially from an aggressive male tiger. But don't be fooled into thinking that an elephant guarantees safety. If the tracker climbs off the elephant, the tiger might charge (or simply flee). Tigers may also take a clawed swipe at the elephant's leg or even prey on a baby elephant if it is away from its mother.

2

IDENTIFY THE TRACKS OF A TIGER

To protect their soft-padded paws from hot and sharp surfaces, for ease of travel, and to find prey, tigers frequently travel on forest trails, riverbanks, dirt roads, and dry streambeds. These predictable locations give the tracker a keen advantage to finding its paw prints, or pugmarks. Look for especially clearly defined and long-lasting prints around waterholes, and always keep in mind that wind, rain, morning dew, and extreme weather conditions—as well as its age—can affect a paw print and make it harder to read. The least likely spots for good prints are grassy and rocky areas.

Like a signature, a paw print's consistent shape and size confirms the tiger's sex, age, and even its identity. The unique pattern of cuts and scars on the tiger's sensitive paws is particularly helpful; it can also reveal an injury. Keep in mind, though, that the same individual's print can look different on different surfaces, especially on dry sand, in which the print may spread.

Tigers walk on their four uniquely shaped toes, which are arranged in a half-circle above a large leathery pad with three roundish lobes at one end. (The fifth toe, like a thumb, is higher on the leg and does not make an impression on the ground.) Their tracks show no claw marks, since their claws are retractable, which helps the tracker distinguish them from those left by a wolf, wild dog, jackal, hyena, sloth bear, or ratel (honey badger).

The paws of a male tiger are squarer and bigger than a female's, and all tigers' front paws (which support the heavier and more muscular part of the body) are about 15 percent larger than their back paws. The male's front paws are about 5.1 inches (13.2 cm); the female's are 4.6 inches (11.8 cm). The pad of a tiger's paw is about 75 percent of its total area, including the toes.

A female's is rectangular with typical dimensions of about 5 inches (13 cm) long by 4.3 inches (11 cm) wide. The male's is shorter—about 4.7 inches (12 cm)—but wider, at about 5 inches (13 cm). The male's back toes are rounder than the female's elongated ones.

Golden rays of the first morning sun highlight a series of paw impressions in the loose dirt in the road. These prints are from a male tiger who walked past at an even pace sometime during the night. Trackers in jeeps look for tiger prints in the road while the elephants sweep the forest and meadow areas, searching for other clues.

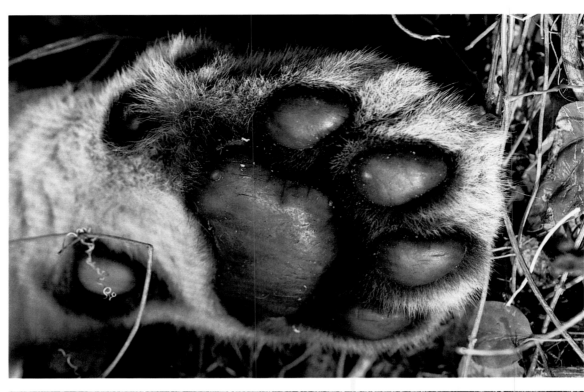

The tigers' toes tell the tracking story. Four toes are arranged in a semicircle above the large, leathery three-lobed pad, with the fifth toe higher on the leg. Check the paw for any unique characteristics that could be left as the tiger walks on its toes silently through the forest. Sometimes, the tracker follows poor paw impressions in hopes of finding better ones when the tiger crosses onto a dirt trail.

Right: Choti independently scouts over Bandhini Hill's cliff edge, scanning the forest below for anything that moves, especially prey. Her paw prints are half the size of her mother's. Be assured, Bachhi is not too far away from her cubs.

Try to focus on one of a tiger's hind paw prints. (You can be sure it's a hind paw print if the third toe protrudes beyond the fourth.) Hind paw prints are clearer and easier to read since the hind paw usually steps into the front paw print. Check the prints over a period of time to confirm the presence of a specific tiger in the area.

And remember to look at the big picture, to attempt to understand individual paw prints in the context of the others in the area.

Figuring the length of a tiger's stride is also useful. Tigers move on both feet on one side at the same time. A male Bengal tiger, whose average stride is about 4 feet (122 cm), is about 10 feet (3 m) long from head to tail tip, and easily weighs about 400–570 pounds (180–258 kg). The average walking stride of a female is about 3 feet (1 m); females' bodies are about 8 feet (3 m) long, and they weigh 220–350 pounds (100–160 kg). The taller the tiger at its shoulder, the longer its stride.

Tracking a Legend

Right: Banda is on a prowl in the deep grasses of the Rajbehra Meadow hunting for chital (spotted deer). Notice how he drops his head to stalk and stride through the grass. Bachhi may traverse his territory, leaving her footprints on the loose dirt trails, as she returns to her cubs in a nearby cave. Bachhi fears for their and even her own safety around any male tiger. Male tigers fiercely patrol their home range (domain). The tracker may take a plaster impression of both Banda's and Bachhi's hind paw prints to confirm their identity at another time when the tiger is not present.

Left: Choti's energetic explorations lead her into a tightly snarled tree. Cubs can get stuck and then whine in distress for their mother to rescue them. Adult tigers, weighing some 300 lbs (140 kg), are selective about the trees they climb. If the way down is too steep, it invites a fatal fall.

Next page: Gliding inside the bamboo thickets the green whip snake (*Ahaetulla prasina*; *dhamin* in Hindi) glides above the tiger cubs, noticing their presence as it travels on to a higher elevation.

TARGET TIGER TERRITORIES

3

By knowing where a tiger lives and hunts, a tracker is more likely to find it. An average tiger needs a territory of about 20–30 square miles (52–78 sq km) or more to be able to secure enough prey to survive. In areas where there is a lot of prey, tigers need less space to survive. If the prey becomes scarce, then a tiger will likely trespass on another's territory out of hunger, inviting life-threatening encounters.

How are tiger territories staked out?

Male tigers of about two years and older live on their own, meeting up with females to mate and with other males to defend their territory. Males select their territories based on the amount of available prey; the more prey there is in an area, the smaller territories can be. A male's home range overlaps those of several females if conditions are good, so in such cases he'll have more potential mates. They usually see other male tigers as potential rivals and may attack them fiercely, occasionally killing them. If you see two different sets of male paw prints converging in the same area, be alert—there may be a tiger fight about to happen.

Tigers clearly mark their territorial boundaries in a language other tigers understand, by using claw marks scented with sweat from their paws and by urine-spraying tree trunks or the underside of low branches with their unique scent.

Males are tolerant of female tigers—sometimes as many as three or more—who have territories overlapping with their own. A very real risk of such shared territory is that the dominant male could perceive the female's sub-adult male cubs as threats and kill them. Cubs can also be at risk if their mothers have intersecting territories, whether they reach into a male's territory or not. Tigresses may not readily share territory with each other and can be aggressive, even if they are sisters.

Cubs usually live with their mothers for about two years, at which point they become independent. Females tend to settle within a home range near their mothers. Young males do not move right into their own territories; they may roam for several years, moving through known territories or struggling to survive in areas with less prey. The alternative is to fight the dominant male tiger for possession of his territory and the females—which means risking injury and even death.

Banda drinks at the waterhole in Rajbehra Meadow after asserting his right to mate with Sita-Wali (Bachhi's sister), whose territory overlaps his own.

3

Tracking a Legend

Banda, the ascendant male, is Bachhi's son from her first litter in 1997. Banda will carry his genes forward as he mates with Sita-Wali. Meanwhile, Charger has lost his mating rights in his own home range as his son, Banda, has asserted his dominance. Male tigers live and hunt alone in their marked territories and enter another tiger's territory at great risk.

Above: Banda mates with Sita-Wali in a surprisingly noisy—and violent—affair.

Right: A male occasionally leaves full-fanged compression bites on the female's neck and comes away from mating with deep claw scratches on his face, from a full-powered sharp-clawed swing that she makes when he releases her. Successful mating will produce a typical litter of two to three cubs about 106 days after conception.

When does tiger mating occur?

Though tiger mating can take place during any season, it most frequently occurs from November to April. When the tigress is in estrus and ready to mate, she attracts the male with frequent scent marks—like a strong jungle perfume—and roars that signal her readiness. Responding male calls can be heard throughout the night. A tiger pair may mate more than a hundred times over five to seven days before the two separate and live solitary lives. Mating looks—and can be—violent and can easily turn into mortal combat. The tigress will mate again only after the cubs have grown—about every two years—or if she loses her cubs.

3

The rules of the jungle show no mercy to the young. When this unlucky eight-month-old male and his mother ventured into Banda's territory in search of prey, Banda killed the potential challenger with one quick bite to the neck. He let the tigress and the cub's sister go free, for now, and left the cub's body for the scavengers.

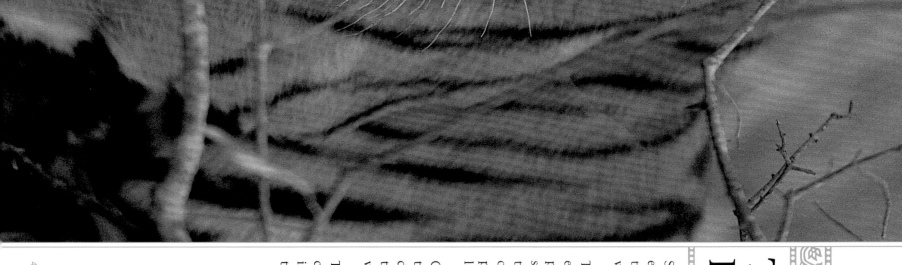

TRACK THE TIGER'S DIRECTION & SPEED

Since visitors are not permitted to sleep in the Bandhavgarh reserve, they enter by jeep in the early morning. The driver often swerves out of the main tracks on the dirt road, slowing down to examine the tiger's nighttime hunting track marks, gathering advance information to share with the mahavat.

Tracks are a great clue to a tiger's speed. Shallow tracks usually indicate a fast pace, while deeper ones mean that the cat is walking in a relaxed way with a smooth gait. Focus on the overall pattern of paw prints as well as their depth. As it walks, a tiger moves the two paws on one side of the body at the same time. In a slow walk, the front paws strike the ground first and then the back paws come in closely behind. In a quick walk, the hind footprints move ahead of the front footprints. In a run, both back paws hit the ground simultaneously, the front paws pulling forward with great force. A normal walking stride leaves a double track, and a run leaves a single track, with one paw landing in the print made by another.

Certain tracking clues can come from a tiger's injuries. An old male tiger wandering through the night was limping from a hind leg injury caused during a territorial fight with a young dominant male, his son. The tracker cautiously followed the marks of the left paw dragging in the dirt to find the direction of the injured tiger to able to assess the seriousness of the injury without any unexpected surprises.

To find the direction and speed of a tigress and cubs, search trails and *nallas* (ravines) to discover a set of smaller paw prints surrounding the tigress' rectangular paw prints. If the tigress is moving slowly, the cubs will play with each other along the way; if she is moving quickly the cubs will stay in a tight formation close to her body.

4

Badi keenly focuses on nearby deer through the tree branches. Her mother, Bachhi, is resting behind a rock from a brief fight with Charger during an evening hunt.

Talking to the Mahavat

dirt road: *sa rak*
stream: *chash-maa*
waterhole: *paanee*
cave: *guhaa*
meadow: *maidaan*
bamboo: *baans*
grass: *ghaas*
forest: *jangal*
village: *gaaon*

4

Left: With a full belly, Choti, who has a heart-shaped stripe on her elbow, wobbles and regains her balance, swinging her tail as she climbs down from a fallen tree to show her independence to her mother. Cubs learn by doing.

Right: Choti (above) struggles up rocky ledges, determined to follow Bachhi up Bandhini Hill, where they'll spend the night. Badi takes a more meandering path, darting through bushes and low-lying trees as she stalks leaves, branches, and anything else that moves.

4

Tracking a Legend

Charger (above) is following Bachhi and her two cubs because he is hungry and is having difficulty catching his own prey. He tries to push Bachhi and the cubs off the prey they caught with intimidating body gestures and a ferocious growl. Charger's tracks are easy to follow because of his injury to his left leg and the drag mark in his print.

To find the direction and speed of a tigress and cubs, search trails and *nallas* (ravines) to discover a set of smaller paw prints surrounding those of the tigress. When she is moving slowly, the cubs will play with each other along the way; if she is moving quickly the cubs will stay in tight formation close to her body.

LOOK FOR TIGER CLAW MARKS

Like posting a "Keep Out" sign, tigers carve long, deep grooves into the trunks of select trees by stretching their forelimbs up the trunks and pulling down, ripping the bark with their powerful claws. Scent-laden sweat secreted from their claws and pads is rubbed into the trees as they scratch. By sniffing the scratch marks, tigers can identify the signs of other tigers that are familiar to them. Unknown tigers in their territory risk being evicted by the resident. The height of the claw marks can help determine the size of the tiger. Don't be confused by the high, short claw marks made by the sloth bear.

The tiger has particularly flexible, swiveling wrists and strong, sharp, and maneuverable claws. It flexes the muscles in its paws to release its retractable claws. Finely honed for hunting, this powerful system gives tigers the first-strike advantage. When they hold on they don't let go. Clawing trees stretches the paw muscles and cleans the claws.

Tracking a Legend

Banda's huge scented claw marks dug into a tree in a *nalla* (ravine) near Bandhini Hill warn other tigers, wildlife, and humans to beware when entering his marked domain. Charger has noticed these new claw markings in his territory. A fight is bound to happen.

5

5

At the age of one week, a tiger cub's claws are not yet retractable, but they are sharp. Over the next few months, the paws will develop the strength and flexibility needed for hunting and traveling in the jungle.

Compare the claw size of a one-week-old tiger cub with that of a seven-month-old. The claws, pads, and overall paw size of the older cub are about four times that of the baby. The younger cub's muscles have not developed enough to allow it to retract its claws. In the tiger's hunt, the fully opened hook-like claws are most critical for grasping its prey. A paw injury could be fatal for a cub if it prevents it from keeping up with its mother.

One-week-old cub's paws and claws

Paws and claws of a seven-month-old cub

SMELL THE SCENT OF A TIGER

6

While traveling on the back of an elephant, you may get a whiff of the pungent pheromone odor of urine-sprayed trees along the forest trails. It's a powerful and lingering ammonia-like smell that tigers use to define their home range. Every tiger has its own clearly identifiable scent. If you smell it strongly, look around: the tiger might be walking or resting very close by. Sometimes, the tracker will smell the tiger just before seeing it. Keep alert for the tiger's stripes, which help it blend into the forest terrain.

Though tigers usually depend on their acute vision and hearing, they often do communicate with each other by using scents. A tiger's "Flehmen face"—with its characteristic wrinkled nose, raised lips exposing the fangs, and tongue hanging out—is the sign of a tiger inhaling a special scent, drawing it into its Jacobson's organ, located in the roof of the mouth. There, a quick chemical translation is done that tells the tiger who has been there (friend or foe), how long ago, and if it's a female, whether she is in heat.

Scents from trees, claw marks, droppings, and even a paw print in the dirt road can produce the primal grimace of the Flehmen face.

A tiger's hairless nose is sensitive to touch and temperature. Some tigers have speckled markings on their nose, which help identify them. The tiger's whiskers are like radar sensors, helping it judge its position, even during the hunt when it is delivering a killing bite.

Tracking a Legend

Charger followed his nose to this strong-smelling carcass Bachhi left half-covered by leaves. He pulls the deer carcass with his front teeth to get the best hold on the food he so needs to help him in his weakened condition. The injuries he incurred from fighting with Banda have made it even harder for him to hunt.

Left, bottom: Banda frequently urine-sprays the territory in which he is currently mating with Sita-Wali. Mating lasts for about five days.

Right: With this Flehmen face, the tiger senses other tigers that have been in the area by their one-of-a-kind scent. The Jacobson organ, located in the roof of its mouth, helps identify the scents.

HUNT FOR TRACES OF THE TIGER

The tiger eats a massive amount of meat. The average tiger kills about fifty deer-sized prey animals a year—one kill every seven or eight days—but a tigress with young cubs may kill as much as 50 percent more a year, eating every five or six days, or more frequently if her feeding with her cubs had been disrupted. Tigers digest food rapidly and their scat (feces) can often be found along the trail, where it may serve as a territory marker. The odor, shape, and contents (for example, chital fur) of the scat tells the tracker what the tiger ate and how long ago it was in the location. Many trackers never see a tiger, but the scat tells them that the animals are in the area.

Look for areas of the ground that have been scraped bare. Tigers often clear the ground around where they defecate, drawing attention to the scent deposit. Scrapes are a useful tracking clue.

Trackers make plaster casts of the tiger's paw prints to record which tigers are in an area and to make note of any peculiar paw pad indentations that help identify a specific tiger. Knowing which tiger is claiming a piece of territory helps establish their pattern of patrolling and hunting, which could help a tracker learn to predict the tiger's habits.

Tracking a Legend

Bachhi and her cubs are eating a spotted deer above their Bandhini Hill cave, trying to hide their prey from such bothersome scavengers as vultures and crows. Bachhi can eat about 40 lbs (18 kg) of meat in one sitting. The cubs also feast on the meat, usually selecting the tender internal organs first.

7

7

Badi eats in peace, putting her head entirely inside the deer carcass and gorging until she's satisfied. When she is finished, Bachhi will lick her face and body thoroughly to clean her cub and reinforce their mother-daughter (family) bond.

Some tiger field biologists capture tigers and put radio collars on them to precisely determine their home ranges and track their movement patterns and diets through different seasons. Highly sensitive cameras, triggered to take a picture anytime a tiger walks down a trail, can be used to capture an image of a tiger's unique face, profile, and striped body pattern. Since the tiger is mostly nocturnal, the nighttime pictures provide an invaluable tool for studying tigers in their own habitat. Researchers can also use DNA analysis of tiger hair and scat to study individual tigers and, potentially, tiger populations.

Tiger tracking can include a mix of traditional and modern techniques. No matter how it's gathered, the information from quality field observations—along with a commitment from the local forest officials and villagers—helps to build a sustainable tiger conservation program.

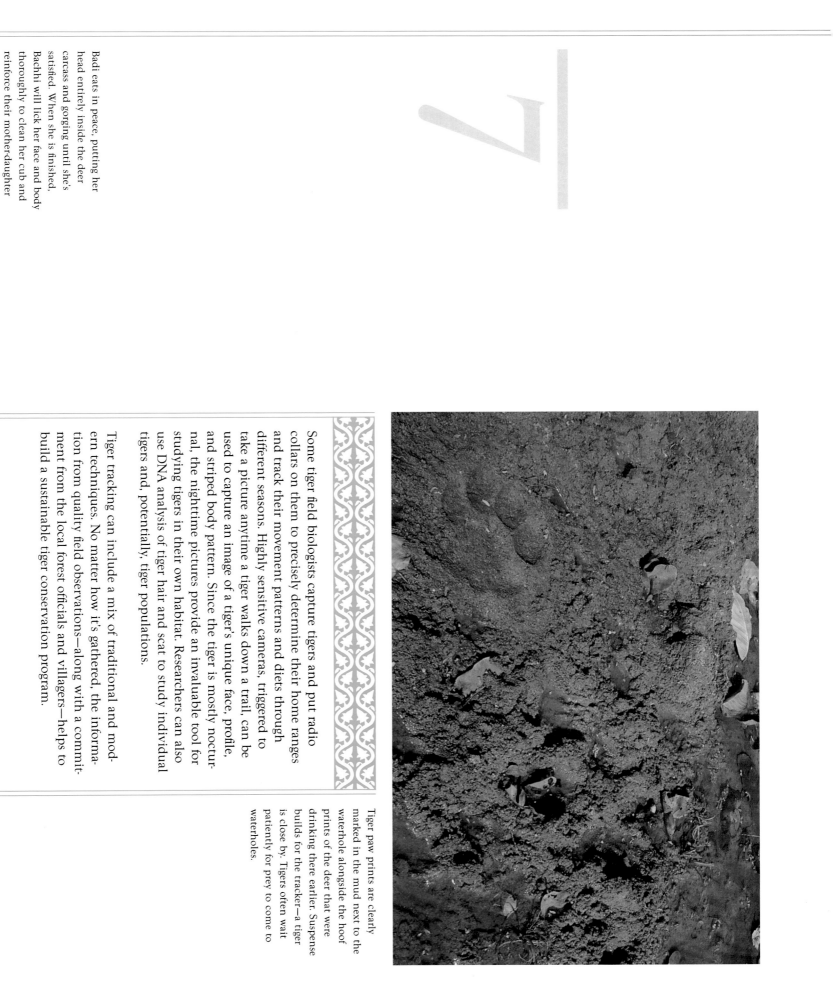

Tiger paw prints are clearly marked in the mud next to the waterhole alongside the hoof prints of the deer that were drinking there earlier. Suspense builds for the tracker—a tiger is close by. Tigers often wait patiently for prey to come to waterholes.

DISCOVER EVIDENCE OF THE TIGER'S NIGHTTIME HUNT

Primetime for hunting tigers is from dusk to dawn. The bulge of a tiger's eye makes it work as a wide-angle lens, picking up much more information than a human eye can. During the day it sees about as sharply as we do and in a limited range of colors (dull blue and green), but its night vision is significantly better—about five to six times better than humans'.

Two anatomical features make this possible: A tiger's retina contains a high number of rod cells, the cells that make black-and-white night vision possible. Also, where humans and other diurnal mammals have a layer of dark pigment cells behind the retina that absorbs extra light, tigers and other nocturnal animals have a reflective layer called the tapetum lucidum. The tapetum bounces the extra light back into the retina, giving the eye a second chance at catching it. The tiger's extraordinary vision gives it a strategic hunting advantage: The darkness can conceal the predator while it spies its prey, stalks, and moves in for the hunt.

If a tracker shines a light into the forest after dark and sees round yellow mirrorlike eyeshine—reflections off the tapetum—with just the right eye spacing, eye size, and height, it means the tiger is right there.

Tigers start hunting in the cool hours of the evening and will continue on and off through the night. Once successful, they'll often briefly rest and then eat the prey; otherwise, they'll continue to prowl through the night—Bengal tigers sometimes traveling as far as 10–20 miles (16–32 km)—and even into the day if they are very hungry. Tigers continue to hunt especially during a full or new moon, even when the prey is better able to see them.

Looking out over the expanse of the tiger reserve from the Bandhavgarh Fort, the Maharaja raises his hand as an evening storm approaches. The jungle nightjar, *Caprimulgus indicus*, signals the transition of dusk to the darkness of night with its repeated *chuckoo-chuckoo*. Disguised by its ashy-brown feathers and close ground nesting, this night bird will launch into flight as the tiger walks by on its hunt.

Next page: Bachhi, with the advantage of her superior night vision, walks the ridge of Bandhini Hill as she hunts by moonlight.

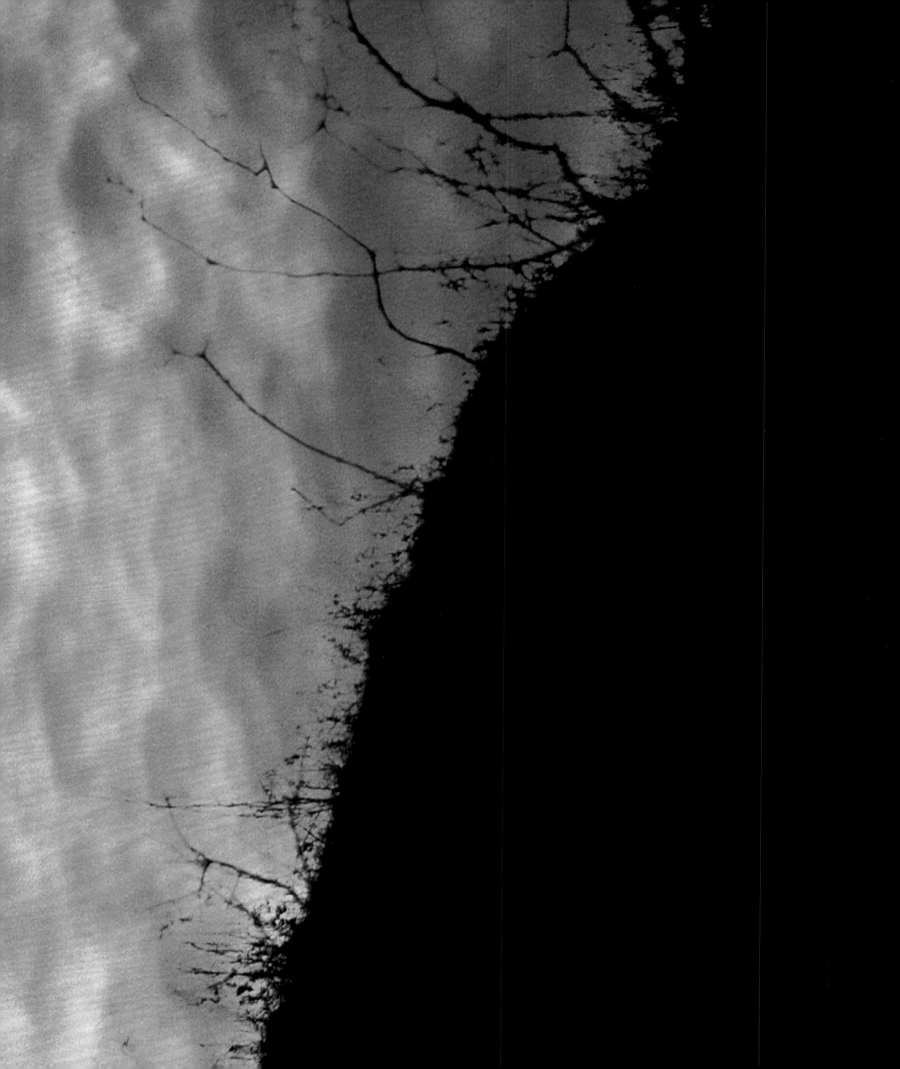

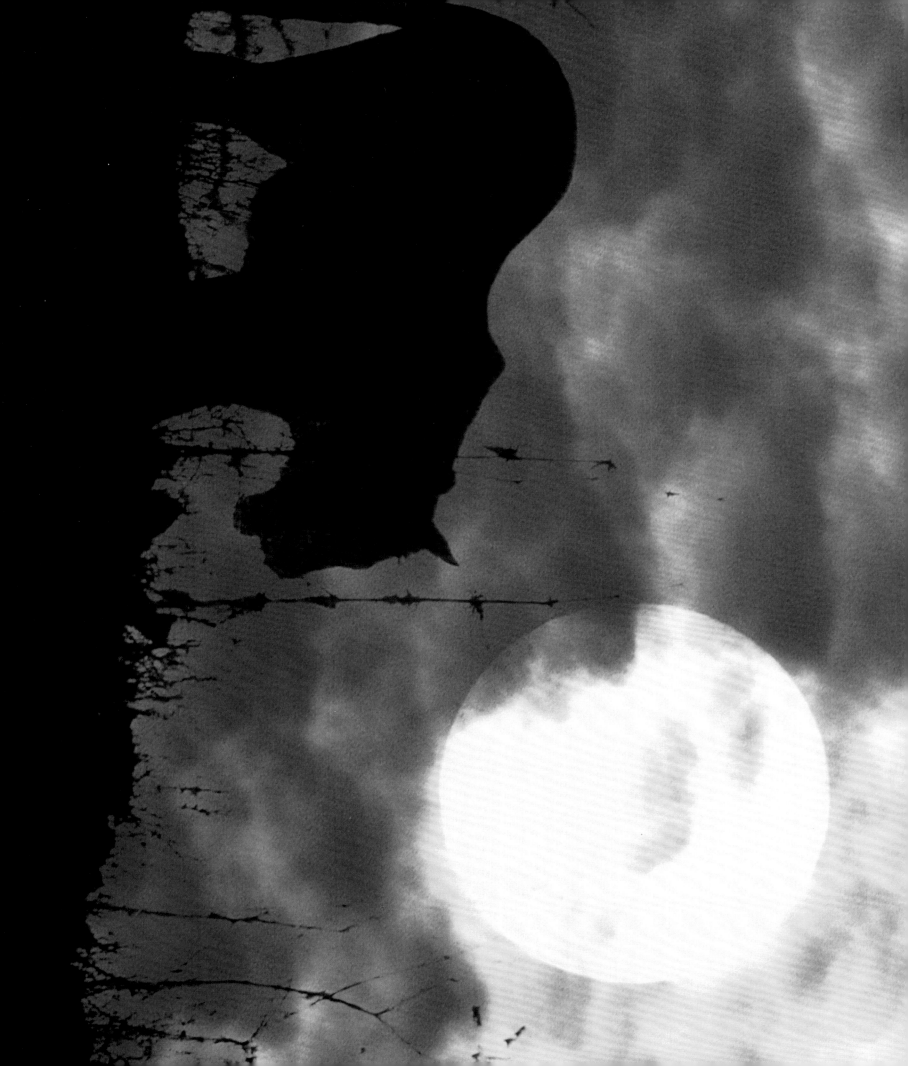

As darkness advances, an everyday drama unfolds for the nervous prey and the hungry predator. A sambar deer drinks at water's edge before going into the forest for the night.

∞

Tracking a Legend

Dayaram and Lalu travel back at dusk to the elephant camp for the night. Bachhi leaves the cubs in a secure cave at night so she can hunt nearby, only about a mile (1.6 km) away. She stays close by to minimize the distance she needs to drag the prey to the cave and the distance the cubs have to travel.

IDENTIFY TIGER MARKINGS

9

A tiger's beauty is in the unlimited combinations of long, swerving stripes, innovative black-lined squiggles, and spots marking its magical red-orange fur. The asymmetrical stripes on each tiger are unique—no two tigers are the same. In the tiger's natural habitat, the stripes blend with the jungle's bamboo, camouflaging the tiger's movements. In addition, the rough, coarse hair of the male's short mane gives it a special distinction.

Every tiger has a different constellation of spots on its face and muzzle, a variable number of striped rings on its tail, and two predictable white spots on the back of its black ears.

A tracker looks quickly for unique stripes on the animal's face, shoulder, legs, and side to easily identify it. (One tiger cub, Choti, had a stripe in the shape of a heart on her front leg, which made it easier to know her when she was with her mother.) Also check to see if any of the tiger's fangs are broken or chipped. Scars and nicks in the ear can often instantly confirm a tiger's identity. The conspicuous scrotum easily distinguishes males from females at a distance.

A tiger's lower face, throat, chest, belly, and inner limbs are usually white or light cream, but don't rely on color too much. One side of the tiger's face and body can be entirely different from the other, and its fur can be bleached from the sun or stained with mud. Also, be attentive to confirming the tiger's real size as it may look different with a full belly or a few days after having eaten.

What's the quickest way to identify a tiger? First, at a distance, check the size of the tiger and the length of its gait. As you approach the cat, look at its striped markings, facial scars, and fur coat condition.

Bachhi's beauty is one of a kind. Her clear facial markings include the spots on her nose, muzzle, and cheeks, and the asymmetrical brush strokes on her forehead, which carry through onto her body. Tiger fur patterns are among the most remarkable of nature's multitude of patterns.

Bachhi left profile

Tracking a Legend

Left: Bachhi, always alert with her cubs nearby, dips down to drink from a low spring near her Bandhini Hill cave area, revealing her muscular build and body stripes. Fights between tigers frequently leave facial scars, permanent wounds on the nose and claw marks on the tiger's tail area. And sometimes the tiger's prey leaves its marks with hoof-kicking scrapes, tusk puncture wounds, tearing horns, bite impressions, and even porcupine quills lodged in a tiger's face. Banda has several deep scars on his nose which can be seen clearly in the photograph on page 134.

Bachhi right profile

Trackers often memorize the pattern of each tiger's right and left facial profile to be able to confirm a tiger's identity. Left: Bachhi's left profile, with its distinct figure-eight design among other stripes. Right: Bachhi's right profile shows an uneven V-shaped squiggle sweeping upward. No two sides—face or body—are alike.

9

Bachhi sits on her haunches, enjoying the cool water and the playful splashing of her cubs at Bandhini Waterhole. Suddenly she hears something strange in the trees—a possible intruder—and looks up with a penetrating stare. A tiger's facial expression, the powerful clarity of its eyes, and its level of alertness can help identify it. The mahavats recognize the trademark facial expressions of certain tigers, like Charger's intensely wrinkled nose combined with a fang-baring growl. Under the shifting shade light of the trees, the often easily identifiable fur patterns of Bachhi and her family could look different than when they are in full sun. Be a detective. Take note of everything about a tiger and its behavior.

As a tiger cools off at the edge of a deep waterhole and a favorite ambush hunting spot, its splendid striped body patterns produce mesmerizing reflections. The tiger's insulating fur helps it maintain a constant body temperature of about 99° F (37° C). The colder the tiger's climate, the longer its hair will be. Tigers shed their coats once or twice a year and have longer fur in the winter and shorter fur in the summer. Their hairs function as a sensory device.

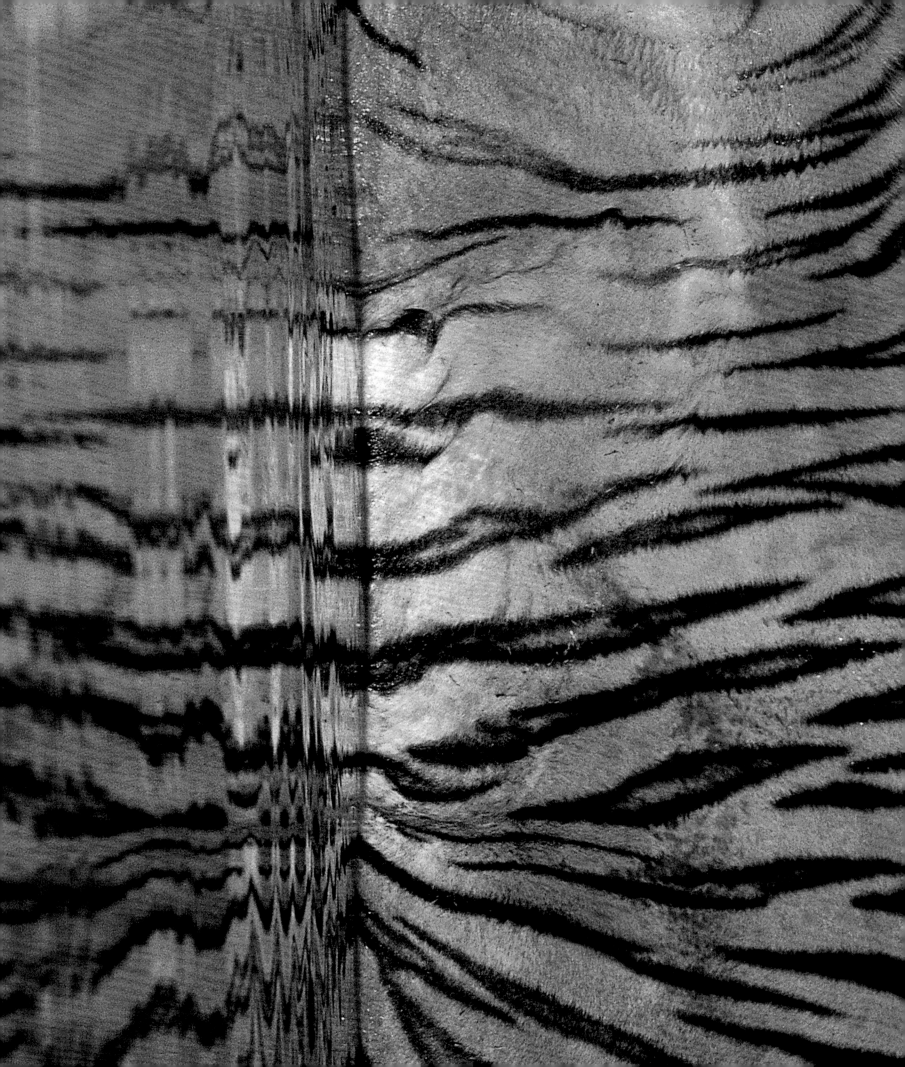

PREDICT THE TRAVELS OF THE TIGRESS AND CUBS

T

After a gestation period of about three and a half months (100–106 days), a tigress gives birth to a litter of usually three or four cubs. The average tigress has three or four litters over her fifteen-year lifespan. It takes about two years to raise the cubs, and the tigress does it alone. Until they are about four to six months old, she nurses them and keeps them sheltered in a series of caves, bamboo thickets, or ravines, moving to a new one every few days to protect the cubs from predators (leopards, snakes, sloth bears, and other tigers) who may smell the cubs. During this time, she goes out at night to hunt for herself to maintain her strength.

The cubs open their eyes six to fourteen days after birth. At about two to three months, you might spot them play-wrestling, but they never go far on their own. Their mother may take them to drink at the nearest waterhole every morning and evening during the intense summer heat, and she will start bringing them to a kill to start eating meat at this point as well. Since they grow rapidly—gaining 3 to 5 pounds (1.3–2.3 kg) a week in their first year—cubs eat meat every two to three days and continue to nurse at least twice a day until they are about six months old. Cubs weigh about 2 to 3 pounds (.9–1.3 kg) at birth and if they have sufficient food they grow to about 150 pounds (68 kg) by one year, becoming potent predators.

While they are growing, the cubs constantly play and stalk each other, learning the fundamental skills of the hunt. Cubs start to hunt under their mother's watchful eye at eleven months. It is crucial that they master the skill by the time they are two years old and separate from her—their survival depends on it.

Keeping track of a tiger's hunger is the best way to predict its movements. Bachhi and the cubs may stay near a kill, if it is a large animal like a sambar, for two or three days.

Bachhi relaxes, breathing deeply, as she nurses her five-month-old cubs, usually twice a day, on an overlook at Bandhini Hill. At the same time, she is vigilant, her watchful eyes scanning for any danger, as she is vulnerable. If she senses anything strange, she jumps to attention, ending the nursing, ready to fight or flee with her cubs.

Tracking a Legend

Badi swings under her mother's chin and gives a brief whining cry to signal that she wants to nurse. Along with eating high-protein meat, drinking the vital body-building milk will accelerate a cub's growth. Bachhi is a true mother: a nurturer, a protector, a teacher, and the cubs' constant companion.

While Bachhi grooms her cubs it reinforces the intimate bonding and nurturing within this tiger family. Each cub has a distinct scent.

How will the tracker most often find the tigress and the cubs?

Look for caves and bamboo thickets near a waterhole especially at dawn or dusk, and try to find paw prints of an adult female with those of cubs. If you spot the tigress moving through the forest, follow her, because she won't be more than a mile away from where the cubs are resting.

Bachhi spends hours each day grooming her cubs. She will lick them clean all over until they can lick themselves. Bachhi is injured from her nighttime hunt and a fight with Charger, whose claw drew blood below her right eye and down her nose.

Left: Twice a day, Bachhi takes her cubs to a small spring near a cave she is using at Bandhini Hill. The cubs take every opportunity to wrestle and play together. Badi uses the full force of her body weight to issue a friendly sisterly bite.

Right: Bachhi tolerantly allows her cub to slide over her back while wrapped around her neck. Frequent touching is reassuring to cubs and an important form of nonverbal communication within the tiger family. Cubs get creative in their play, often going for their mother's safe swinging tail as if it were prey. Her tail becomes a target to practice the hunt.

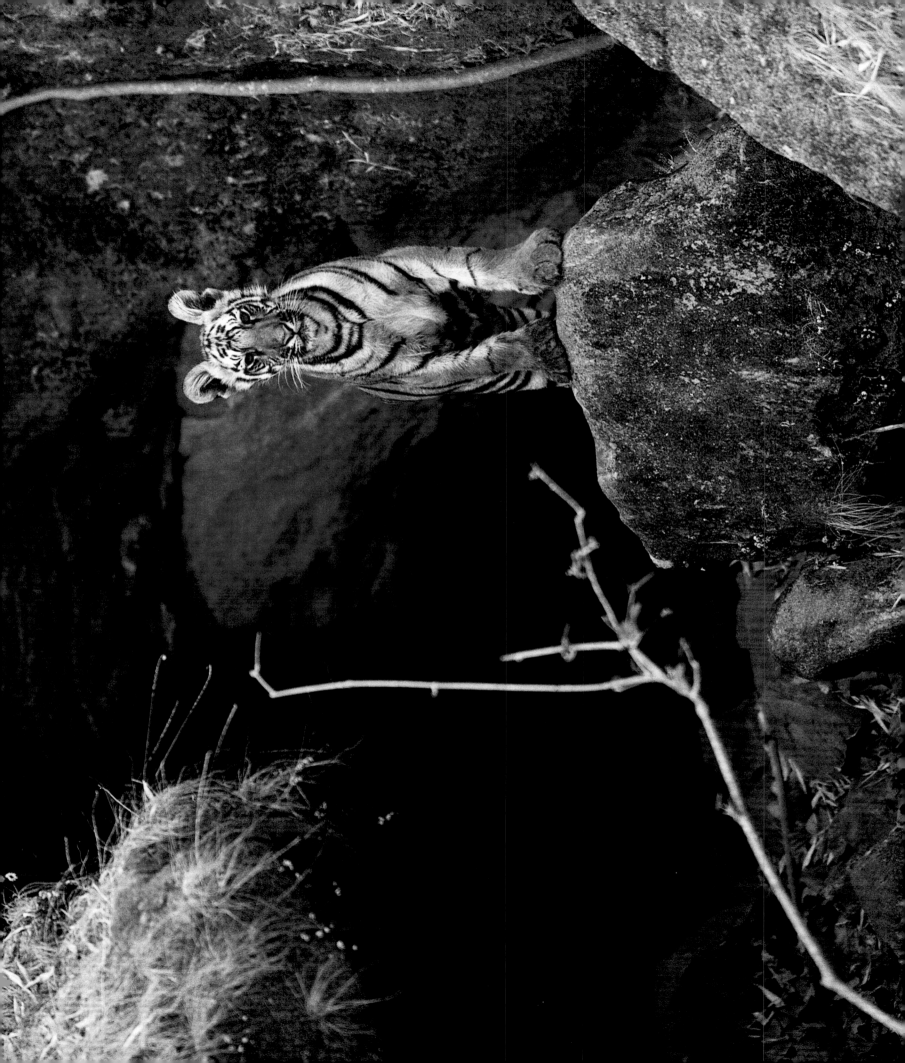

EXPLORE THE TIGER'S COOL CAVES

T

During the extreme heat of the summer months—from March through June temperatures can reach 110° F/43° C—tigers like to take shelter in cool caves during the heat of the day. If you know the location of a favorite cave (*guhaa* in Hindi), you'll be able to look inside from atop an elephant or simply wait for the tiger to emerge, often at dusk when the tiger visits a waterhole. Watching the cave area helps you determine the tiger's next move, whether it's hunting or quenching its thirst at the waterhole.

Observe the cave from outside only, and do not get off the elephant! Leave the tigers enough space to easily come and go. And don't ever enter the cave. Inside, you might be surprised by a tiger, sloth bear, leopard, python, or even a poisonous cobra.

As a reminder of how tigers and humans shared this land, you can sometimes see a tiger resting in the entrance of a sandstone cave directly in front of first-century BC Brahmi inscriptions.

Tigers are light sleepers, frequently opening their eyes to scan their surroundings. They can leap to their feet at a moment's notice. Based on this behavior, they sometimes rest on expansive rocky cliffs to have a panoramic view of what might be approaching.

Tiger caves range from simple concavities in rock walls to various sizes of corridors opening into cavernous interiors, even some ancient manmade caves. The best caves are high up on the north side of hills, away from the afternoon sun, with a waterhole nearby. They give the tiger a good vantage point for scanning for prey or threats, as well as a safe place to eat, rest after a night of hunting, recover from injury or birth, and raise cubs. During monsoon season, lower caves often flood, forcing the tigers to seek higher ground.

In the cooler months, tigers abandon their caves and stay in the tall grasses and bamboo bushes and thickets.

Badi tumbles out of the Bandhini Hill cave with zeal to greet her mother after hearing her deep bellowing calls, which travel for miles in the jungle. She scrambles on top of a boulder lookout at the cave's entrance while her sister, Choti, is waking up inside the cave.

Left: Bandhini Hill's many caves are carved high on the face of the cliff, creating resting spots that allow Badi to catch a cool breeze, keep away from predators, and have an ideal vantage point from which to watch a wide range of wildlife in the jungle, especially any coming near her space.

Right: Badi and Choti walk along the cave's cliff face "catwalk" and settle down in the "air-conditioned" recesses of the cave to escape the heat. The cubs use their tails to help them keep their balance, and they sometimes flick them to communicate with each other. A tiger's tail grows to be about 3 feet (1 m) long and is usually marked with eight to twelve distinct rings.

11

Tracking a Legend

Caves are never permanent homes for tigers; they're for short stays only. In the summertime, tigers use the many Bandhavgarh caves to shelter from the sun, to eat their prey without being bothered by scavengers, and to rest and recover from an injury made by another tiger or during a rough hunt. One day when Banda returned to Rajbehra Cave to find it occupied by Charger, they both unleashed loud snarls and growls in a turf battle. Dayaram and his elephant, Wanraj, were nearby and became frightened by the loud sounds of the hissing and roaring cats. Wanraj screeched and ran away in the mayhem, with Dayaram temporarily losing control.

After eating a wild boar he dragged to Thaudi Cave, Banda is resting in the golden sunset light. This hunt represented one of Banda's first successful and most needed hunts after he separated from his mother, Bachhi.

Left: Bachhi rests in a cool cave at the base of Bandhini Hill, always ready to rescue her daredevil cubs who climb the nearby rock ledges with boundless energy.

12

KEEP TRACK OF TIGER CUBS

Because of their size, the paw prints made by a tiger cub are relatively easy to tell from those made by an adult, but be careful not to be misled by leopard prints, which are also small. Just keep in mind that even the largest leopard paw print—about 3–4 inches (8–10 cm)—is smaller than that of even a three-month-old tiger.

Tiger cub tracks are usually found in sets that include its mother's rectangular paw prints. A tiger cub is usually very active, playing, running, jumping—leaving its prints all over a trail and dirt area. If you find a set of unaccompanied small cat prints, they are more likely to be from a leopard. Also, check the length of the cat's stride. A full-grown male leopard's stride is much longer than that of a small tiger cub.

If you see male paw prints on top of those of a tigress and cubs, it may signal that the male is following, and a conflict might result. Other dangers may come from another tigress with cubs in the area. If the tigress is a first-time mother she may not be fully alert to the threats to the cubs.

A growing tiger moves from complete dependence to independence, going through many developmental stages, much like a human child. When cubs emerge from their caves at about three months, they stick very close to their mother, communicating with gestures and unique vocal cues like affectionate chuffing. Cubs can offer a full range of hisses, snarls, and growls to object to things, but their mother always has the final disciplinary growl. They stick together, with the tigress clearly in control, until the cubs are about two years old, when they go off on their own completely.

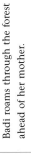

Badi roams through the forest ahead of her mother.

Tracking a Legend

When Bachhi is resting after a meal, Badi decides to return to the kill on her own to continue eating. Bachhi is not far away and always rests with one eye out for any trouble a cub might encounter. She is often most concerned with the presence of an aggressive tiger. Half of all tiger cubs die before the age of six months.

Badi bites and wrestles a branch out of her way in the forest. Through time and experience, this curious cub becomes increasingly bold in everything she does, from learning to hunt to making her own way through the jungle.

Next page: Badi and Choti lead the way down a forest trail on Bandhini Hill as they go to the waterhole.

12

BE ALERT FOR THE TIGER'S PREDATORS

Tigers must beware of predators on the prowl—including Indian leopards, sloth bears, Indian wolves, and reticulated pythons—whether they are in a cave, a forest, a meadow, or at the waterhole.

Indian Leopard (Panthera pardus) (tendwa, chita—Hindi)
Highly adaptable, Indian leopards tend to set up their territory at the edge of a tiger's or simply stay out of the way, but they do occasionally cross into tiger territory to hunt. A female leopard may take on this task because she needs to eat to keep up her strength to nurse and feed her own cubs, usually two to a litter. Leopards have a large menu of selections, including birds, reptiles, fish, and mammals—including tiger cubs and occasionally humans. After killing its prey, a leopard can be run off by wolves, wild dogs, striped hyenas, or a tiger.

The leopard—about one-third the weight and one-fourth the size of a tiger—has the strength of a body builder. It can carry twice its weight up into a tree, where it eats in peace, unmolested by adult tigers. When tracking a leopard, look in trees and in the grasses for its distinctive black rosette spots, shaping unique patterns all over its short-haired tan body. Leopards and tigers share many of the same trails.

At night, leopards can be heard before they are seen. Their distinctive breathing sounds like a raspy chainsaw. Once you've heard that sound, you will never forget it. The leopard is silent during the hunt.

Indian Wolf (Canis lupus)(bheriya, nekra—Hindi, north-central India)
(not illustrated) The Indian wolf is a professional nighttime hunter but will often hunt in the day to avoid the tiger, as they are after the same prey. However, while the tiger hunts solo, the wolf hunts in pairs or in packs, keeping its long muzzle down on the trail to find and follow the scent of its prey. Its long, erect ears serve like a radar-warning device to guide it. Sometimes wolf tracks—with the marks of their straight, blunt, and non-retractable claws—converge with tiger tracks in the jungle, because a pack of wolves will fight a tiger, especially if a den of pups is nearby. When this happens, there will be casualties on both sides. Wolves' relatives, Indian wild dogs—*dhole* in Hindi) can tirelessly outrun their prey, no matter its size, and are thus a danger to tigers and cubs, particularly if they are out in the daytime.

13

Tracking a Legend

This Indian leopard is hungry and hunting at the edge of the forest in the Rajbehra Meadow, Banda's prime tiger territory. The leopard—a rare sight in tiger territory—is waiting for its opportunity to strike at a chital stag. He is gambling that he'll be able to make the kill, eat it quickly, and escape without Banda noticing.

13

Indian Leopard Hunt in Tiger Territory

Left: This male leopard's hunger has driven it from the fringes of a tiger's territory right into its prime hunting meadows. Usually nocturnal, a leopard is hunting in the daytime to avoid a tiger. Such an encounter could prove fatal unless the leopard is able to escape up a tree and stay put a long while. This leopard was successful hunting and straddles its prey much as a tiger does, to quickly drag it from the meadow to the forest's edge, where it will eat. Next time, a wandering tiger cub far from its mother could be its target.

Sloth Bears (Melursus ursinus) (bhalu—Hindi, north India)

The sloth bear defends its territory and hates surprises like curious wandering tiger cubs. The bears are extremely territorial and will respond to any intruder with growls of varying degrees of ferocity, depending on their level of surprise; mothers with cubs can be particularly dangerous. Sloth bears have blackish-brown unkempt fur with a V-shaped breast patch and long ivory-white claws. These medium-sized bears usually search for food all night and sleep near a tree or rock outcropping during the day. Their favorite food is termites and other insects, but they enjoy fruit in the hot season.

Never get between a sloth bear and its food. This is a lesson many villagers have learned, since they share the bear's passion for mahua fruit. They fear the sloth bear even more than the tiger because the bears don't hesitate to attack, maul, and even kill people. The tiger respects the sloth bear, fearing injury from its ferocious bites and gripping claws.

Sloth bears are designed to climb using their gripping padded feet, powerful limbs, and strong claws. This female gives her two cubs a ride through the forest. A sloth bear mother is ferocious and could easily attack if threatened. When the tiger tracker sees sloth bear track marks crossing the tracks of the tigress and cubs, there is reason to be concerned for the safety of the tiger cubs.

Venomous snakes, such as the Indian cobra (above), spectacled cobra, and the Indian krait, may pose a deadly threat to tiger cubs, who may pounce on them in a mistaken moment of playfulness. The cobra's hiss warns an intruder that it is too close before delivering a poisonous bite. The Hindi word for "cobra" is *naag*.

Right: This reticulated python is about 20 feet (6 m) long and has just unhinged its jaws to allow it to swallow a deer it caught and suffocated while it was drinking at the waterhole. The python catches the scent of the tiger cubs by tasting the air with its sensitive tongue.

Reticulated Python (*Python reticulatus*) (*ajgar—Hindi*)

Hunting pythons patiently wait for prey, including tiger cubs, to come to the waterhole. Inexperienced cubs might try to tackle a moving python or try to obtain an easy meal by stealing a deer already inside the python. After catching and swallowing its prey, the python needs a safe place to hide while it digests, sometimes for more than two weeks. Avoid termite mounds, hollow logs, or the cool refuge of caves, which are all favorite python hideouts. To track or identify a python, check for the pattern of movement it leaves in the dirt, resembling a series of small scalloped mounds. Found only in southeast Asia, reticulated pythons (also known as regal pythons) are the longest snakes in the world, sometimes over 30 feet (9 m) long.

13

IDENTIFY TIGER SOUNDS

Panthera tigris, the tiger's Latin name, means "roaring tiger." Big cats are able to roar due to the structure of their hyoid, a flexible system of small bones in their throat; domestic cats, whose hyoids are rigid, can merely meow.

But tigers can do a lot more than roar. They communicate with each other using ten to fifteen other distinct sounds, including snarling, hissing, moaning, grunting, growling, roaring, and affectionate chuffing. Each cub has its own distinct vocabulary that it uses with its mother and siblings, often incorporating some of its mother's sounds and calls as it grows. Each mother knows the calls of her cubs, especially any distress call.

The tiger's ears rotate like radar equipment to track the source of every sound, which enables the cats to find each other and their prey. The flexible cartilage under the tiger's ears allows for these rapid discriminating movements.

Unlike adult humans, who are able to hear sounds between about 20 cycles per second (very long wavelengths) and about 15,000 cycles per second (very short wavelengths), tigers are able to hear ultrasonic sounds (frequencies well above the highest that humans can hear). Due to their large middle ear, tigers are able to hear very low frequency sounds much better than humans. Because tigers can produce roars that contain energy in the infrasound range (sounds below the lowest frequency that humans can hear) scientists think that they are probably able to hear infrasounds, as elephants can, as far as four or five miles away! It is safe to estimate that tigers can hear over a frequency range that is two to three times greater than humans'.

Tiger Language

Territorial Roar

As a tiger roams through its territory on its night patrol, it sometimes issues a loud roar that means "I am here." Tigers hunt silently but might roar after catching prey.

Mating Roar

Tiger mating is noisy business. As a tigress searches for a mate she calls with repeated moaning roars at night—these loud roars can carry 3 miles (5 km). The male may respond with a roar of his own or simply seek her out. The male mounts her, half growling and biting her neck, and then finishes with a loud roar. The tigress roars quickly in response.

Badi deeply wrinkles her nose and raises her lip and her tongue to deliver a combination high-pitched hiss, snarl, and growl, along with all the intimidation her tiny fangs can muster. At the same time, her ears rotate back, showing her agitation. Bachhi recognizes the cub's distress call and is approaching at a run.

14

Tracking a Legend

Bachhi and Choti affectionately chuff, affirming their bond as the tigress grooms her cub. When the cub's sound turns to what's best described as a whine, the tigress continues with her work and utters a series of low-pitched guttural sounds that the cub understands.

All-Clear Roar

A tigress makes a repeated low roar to call her cubs from the cave as she approaches. This roar can be heard about a mile (1.6 km) away. At other times she gives a low brief moaning—almost a grunt—to announce her presence.

Affectionate Chuffing

As a form of greeting, especially between a mother and her cubs, a tiger expels air through its lips and nose to make this sound. The other tiger responds by chuffing back and then they affectionately touch and lick each other's faces, sometimes rubbing their bodies under each other's chins while still chuffing. Chuffing also can signal that a cub wants to nurse.

Distress Call

If a cub is threatened or in need of reassurance, it will make a high-pitched distress call that the tigress and siblings will recognize. The mother will race to the cub's defense.

Wrestling Sounds

The sounds of cubs wrestling include short growls interspersed with pauses for biting each other. Quick growls with the snap of a paw usually mean one cub's temporary dominance.

Guttural Growls

These growls sound like an idling motorcycle engine and are a serious warning to others. A repeated growl signals a high degree of agitation. The tiger could easily spring forward in an attack.

Moaning and Grunting

Tigers grunt or moan with an extended, deep low-frequency sound as a way of expressing frustration.

Whining

A frustrated tiger might whine, just like a human child, if it wants something—food, water, its mother's attention—but can't have it right away.

Pooking

This sound is similar to the alarm call of a sambar deer, the tiger's favorite prey, and may be used to communicate alarm or just to indicate the tiger's presence.

The tiger's roar produces low-pitched (infrasonic) sound that can penetrate a dense forest or hilly terrain. The vibrations are like those made by huge subwoofer speakers at a rock-and-roll concert. The roar travels farther in hot temperatures.

LISTEN FOR WILDLIFE ALARM CALLS

Every sound in the jungle has meaning. Each is a clue for the tracker as well as for other wildlife to what is happening around them. Since the deer and the wild boar are the tiger's favorite prey, their alarm calls can often help identify the tiger's direction so others can move away.

What is the most frequent sequence of alarm calls heard when a tiger is sighted?

There is a symphony of uneasy sounds that occur in a well-known sequence as the tiger approaches: First the monkeys bellow from the treetops, then the meadow ground birds—like the red-wattled lapwing and peacock—join in, and next the chital, barking deer, sambar, and wild boar sound off based on their level of perceived threat from a stalking or a traveling tiger.

Black-Faced Langur (Presbytis entellus) (langur, hanuman—Hindi)

When a tiger moves through the forest, blackfaced langurs usually spot it first and sound the alarm with repeated hollow coughs and bellowing calls. When a leopard is nearby, the monkeys' screeches grow even more frantic, since leopards can easily climb trees to catch them. Because of their weight, adult tigers rarely climb trees.

Rhesus Macaque (Macaca mulatta) (bandar—Hindi)

Rhesus monkeys have distinct orange-reddish fur on their sides and rump and live near rocky areas. Troops of them feed on insects, spiders, and plants on the ground. They are quick to spot a tiger's movements and sound a repeated alarm call as they move into the trees for safety.

Chital (Axis axis) (chital—Hindi)

The spotted deer, or chital, will stamp its forefoot and then sound an alarm with a high-pitched bark for even small disturbances. The other nervous deer raise their heads in unison and join in with a chorus of alarm calls.

15

A chital stag sounds the alarm to the herd, stomping his hoof as a tiger approaches the Chorbehra Waterhole.

Black-faced langur

Rhesus macaques

Tracking a Legend

Left: Badi and Choti, constant companions, rest and explore in a bamboo thicket while waiting for their mother's return from a hunt. Black-faced langurs (above) bellow at them from the trees, letting the entire jungle know of their presence. Black-faced langurs get particularly loud and bare their fangs when a leopard is in the area, since leopards can climb trees to capture them in their own safe haven. Rhesus macaques (right) roam in troops, feeding on the forest floor or resting on low branches, taking time to nurse their clinging young. They give a chorus of high-pitched cries heard throughout the jungle when danger is near.

15

Red-Wattled Lapwing (Vanellus indicus) (lal tethari—Hindi)
Yellow-Wattled Lapwing (Vanellus malabaricus) (pela tethari—Hindi)

The red- or yellow-wattled lapwing gives an excited alarm call at the slightest threat of danger in its meadow habitat, especially when standing guard over its ground nesting area. It also may fly over a tiger, calling. The sharp alarm calls sounds continue until the intruder leaves.

Peacocks (Pavo cristatus) (moor—Hindi)

Peacocks have a loud, distinctive may-aw alarm call that carries through the jungle.

Sambar (Cervus unicolor) (sambar—Hindi)

Page 124: Sambars give the most reliable alarm call, a squealing high-frequency bark. All wildlife in the jungle (including mahavats) pay close attention. If the sambar repeats an alarm call, potential trouble is present.

Barking Deer (Muntiacus muntjak) (kakar—Hindi)

Page 125: The muntjac, or barking deer, gives out a series of short, doglike barks when alarmed or in flight, offering early warnings of danger in the forest.

Wild Boar (Sus scrofa) (suar, barba—Hindi)

Page 110: When the wild boar senses danger with its sharp sense of smell, it grunts and squeals as its black bristly mane rises from the nape of its neck all the way to its hindquarters.

Left: The scolding calls of the red-wattled lapwing guarding her newborn chick signal the approach of a tiger crossing the Chakradhara Meadow. This valuable tracking clue helps determine the tiger's direction as it slinks through the tall meadow grasses.

Right: The male peacock's open feather fan advertises his interest in mating with females in the meadow. He needs to keep careful watch to be sure that a tiger doesn't make a meal of him. A peacock's loud call pierces through the jungle.

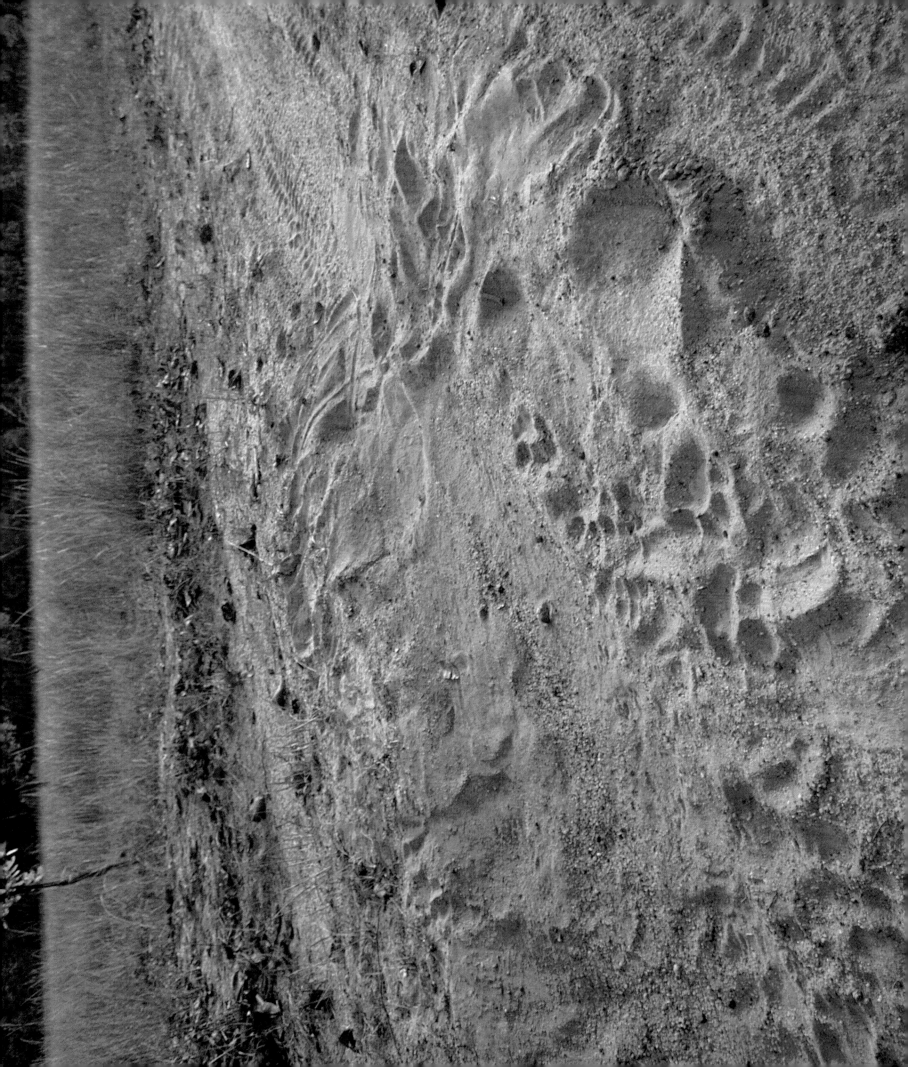

LOOK FOR SIGNS OF CAPTURED PREY

Many tigers and prey animals walk on the dirt roads and trails at dusk and at night for ease of travel through the jungle, so the roads can often be a danger zone. Look for prints and scrapes in the dirt that indicate that a struggle occurred. You may also find clues to the type of prey that was involved.

The successful hunt for a rabbit or other small animal would most commonly result in a tiger's quick bite, snapping the animal's spine, and then the tiger would carry off the prize to eat in the grass, leaving some or no drag marks. If a tiger attacks a male sambar or other large animal, you would find evidence of a significant amount of struggle and long, grooved drag marks from the prey's hooves, antlers, or horns. In addition, you might spot the deep paw prints created when the tiger straddles the animal's body and pulls it into the underbrush to cover it with leaves to hide it from vultures, jackals, and other tigers.

Tigers are extremely possessive of their prey and will most likely return to eat later in the day or after dark, even if they have already eaten a large amount. A tigress may return in the early morning with her cubs, so they can feed or even rest nearby, unless disturbed.

How can the smell of the prey guide the tracker to the tiger's hidden food?

The forest leaves may camouflage a dead deer from prying eyes, but its pungent smell is impossible to mask, especially after one or two days. Swarming flies also signal its location, as do cawing jungle crows, who often find the dead prey first.

Tracking a Legend

The tracks in the dirt road tell the story of Banda's struggle with a chital. The deer's legs and hooves left drag marks leading into the grasses of the Rajbehra Meadow, where the carcass was hidden from scavengers so Banda could eat and rest.

16

T6

Left: A tiger hides the carcass of a chital in the Charanganga Stream and will return with her cubs to eat and cool off in the water later. A leopard passed by and was tempted by the kill, but sensed the tiger's presence and quickly headed for hilly terrain.

Right: Bachhi ate first, making it easier for her two growing cubs to feed on the open carcass. The cubs jostle for the best position and dominance over the carcass. Bachhi scans for any intruders as they eat.

FOLLOW SCAVENGERS

Scavengers—single-minded in their hunt for dead animals to feed on—may lead trackers to a tiger because they are often the first in the jungle to know when a tiger has caught prey. Fiercely intent on their goal, scavengers often compete viciously with each other. Keep your eyes to the sky to watch for vultures.

Black Vulture (*Sarcogyps calvus*) (*gheda—Hindi*) White-Backed Vulture (*Gyps bengalensis*) (*chamar gheda—Hindi*)

Vultures, circling or congregated in a tree, are one of the best daytime signals that a tiger or other predator has recently made a kill. The moment a tiger leaves, vultures descend on the scene. Sometimes, the eerie screeching and flapping noises of vultures and the yelping barks of jackals—also early scavengers—signal the location of the kill. Travel by elephant to witness the vultures-jackal food fights, and search for the tiger nearby as well.

Indian Jackals (*Canis aureus linnaeus*) (*gidhar—Hindi*)

Jackals are swift and can clean a carcass most efficiently. Two hungry jackals will zoom in on a feeding tiger or flock of vultures to take some food for themselves and their pups. The jackal yelps at the screeching vultures or the tiger's annoyed growls, which can be heard through the jungle. As the jackals and vultures are busy fighting, a swift ruddy mongoose (*Herpestes smithi*) dives into the tiger's kill for a quick grabbing bite and then dashes away, in a great escape. The jackal is usually nocturnal, yet on hot days will come out in search of water and any favorable food finds.

Tracking a Legend

After Banda has abandoned his kill, perhaps under pressure from scavengers, a pair of hungry jackals moves in to claim some food for themselves and their pups. Vultures hop closer to the prey and slice at it with their sharp, hooked beaks, all the while fighting with the jackals.

17

Indian Wild Boar (*Sus scrofa*) (*saur, barba—Hindi*)

The boar is omnivorous, usually preferring to eat roots, tubers, and insects, but its extremely keen sense of smell will lead it to a tiger's hidden kill, where it will scavenge and even stand up to the tiger with determination, using its goring tusks defensively. It is braver at night, often staying under cover of bushes and palms as it moves toward the tiger's feast. Follow the wild boar and its powerful sense of smell to find the tiger's prey.

Striped Hyenas (*Hyaena hyaena*) (*hundar, lakkar baghar—Hindi*)

(not illustrated) Indian hyenas are best known as bone-crushing scavengers with extraordinarily powerful jaws and large molars. They live on the prey other animals kill and rely on intimidation to scatter other nighttime scavengers, like jackals. If a tiger takes the possession of its prey seriously, hyenas will usually back off. Hyena paw prints are easily followed since they walk on their four clawed toes, leaving deep impressions.

Jungle Crows (*Corvus macrorhynchos*) and Indian Tree Pies (*Dendrocitta vagabunda*)

(not illustrated) The harsh caws and croaks of these birds travel through the forest, signaling a tiger's location. When the tiger takes a break from eating, these winged carnivores will dare to scavenge a morsel or two, much to the tiger's annoyance.

How do scavengers lead the tracker to the tiger?

Vultures and jackals are the first to arrive at a tiger's kill. They expertly maneuver close to the tiger and disrupt the predator's meal, causing raucous food fights. The vultures' screeching, jackals' yelping, and tiger's annoyed roars carry far and wide and help the tracker locate the kill and the tiger.

Left: A wild boar wallows in a mud bath at Chorbehra Waterhole, where the tigers also drink every day. The wild boar's acute sense of smell can tell it when a tiger is approaching so it can make its retreat.

Right, top: A black vulture posts its lookout on a dead tree branch near the tiger's prey. Soon it and other vultures will descend to pressure the tiger to give up its prey. Badi growls at the vulture and will help her mother defend the food.

14

Left: The Bengal monitor lizard (*Varanus bengalensis*) is a hunter and scavenger with a keen sense of smell that leads it to carrion—especially a tiger's kill in the forest. With a brown scaly body about 3 feet (1 m) long, it whips its tail to throw others off balance and bites with razor teeth holding deadly infection-ridden bacteria. A monitor bite to a tiger cub would cause a slow, painful death.

Right: Looking up through the maze of bamboo, Badi gives a growling squeal to let a fast-moving monitor lizard know she sees it. The lizard is hunting the parrots nesting above as well as scavenging the tiger's kill hidden below.

WATCH THE WATERHOLES

Water (*pannee* in Hindi) is the life source of the jungle. Like pilgrims, the tiger and its prey pay daily visits to the waterhole, but every visit presents the risk of ambush. During the dry summer season, every animal in the jungle gets severely thirsty and has to take its chances at the waterhole or it will die.

Waterholes are the most reliable place to find tigers, as they visit every evening and morning to quench their thirst or rest in the water. Waterholes are also the tiger's favorite site to ambush prey. The nearby bamboo thickets, deciduous trees, and swampy grassland provide a diverse diet for the prey and the perfect camouflage for the predator. To cool down after the hunt, tigers sometimes eat their prey in the water or at its edge.

Unlike most other cats, tigers love the water. They learn to swim at about three months using their powerful front paws and spend many hours drinking, playing, and later even hunting in water. The tigress usually introduces the young cubs to water at a small, shallow spring with easy access and a good view of any approaching predators. Tigers are known to swim long distances, as much as 5 miles (8 km), even from island to island.

Tiger cubs love to mud-wrestle, sliding, tumbling, leaping, rolling, and flinging mud into the air at the same time they deliver a friendly bite to their siblings' hind legs or neck. Some sibling rivalry for dominance is present in these scuffles, but they are mostly mock fights preparing the cubs for future hunting.

Mud offers relief from the heat of the harsh sun by cooling and acting as a sunscreen; it also serves as a parasite remover for the tiger, elephant, and many other species. Mud is also good first aid, keeping flies off and sealing an open wound caused by claws in a fight or unfortunately lodged porcupine quills. As the tiger rolls and lies in the mud near the water's edge, no other wildlife will approach the water to drink except the elephant.

Banda's shimmering silhouette in the Rajbehra Waterhole portrays the essence of a tiger as a hunter, exhibiting a readiness to ambush at a moment's notice.

18

Left: Water is the only relief from the scalding summer heat. Bachhi, her cubs, and most other jungle wildlife must visit the waterhole at least once a day. When the tigers come, everyone scatters and stays clear.

Right: The mahavat's elephant takes a midday break, stretching his legs across the stream and splashing water next to the Bathan elephant camp. After bathing, the elephant throws dust on his back with his trunk for protection from the sun and to keep parasites away.

18

For curious mud-wrestling cubs, the movement of a gigantic reticulated python is an irresistible temptation. But one swat from a playful paw and the snake might strike, killing the cub in its suffocating grip. This snake isn't hungry, its belly still distended with the remains of its last victim, a chital deer. It will continue to digest that meal for two weeks. So for now the cubs are safe, free to pursue their games.

18

Drinking hurriedly, Banda cups his tongue to lap water into his mouth.

Tracking a Legend

Water is the only relief from the scalding summer heat. Banda (left) and Charger (above) had a tense face-off at the Akela Kunda Waterhole early in the day. Charger decided to backtrack, following Bachhi and her cubs' scent, hoping for food from prey Bachhi may have hunted recently.

FOLLOW WILD DEER HERDS

19

Scouting the favorite meadows or waterholes of wild deer often provides exceptional opportunities to spot stalking tigers at dawn and dusk. Follow their tracks, and look for tiger prints nearby. Wild deer love to feast on the blossoms and fruit of trees like the mahua at the edge of the meadow and throughout the forest, and are reluctant to stray far from such treats. Tigers stage ambushes by the fruit trees to catch chital, their favorite prey.

Sambar (Cervus unicolor) (sambar—Hindi)

The largest Indian deer, the sambar stands at 5 feet (1.5 m) high, and large stags, which have antlers, weigh in at 500–700 pounds (225–315 kg). The sambar's coat is brown, tinged with yellow or gray. Sambars usually travel in groups of four to twelve and emerge from the heavy forest cover at dusk. For a tiger, killing a sambar means it will have food for two to three days.

Chital (Axis axis) (chital—Hindi)

Standing about 36 inches (90 cm) high and weighing about 180 pounds (82 kg), the chital, or spotted deer, has light-brown fur and a wide array of white spots; only the stags have antlers. Chital often graze in meadows at dawn and dusk and move into the relative safety of the forest at night. They become an especially easy target of tigers while they are distracted during mating season.

Indian Bison (Bos gaurus) (gaur—Hindi)

(not illustrated) A small seasonal herd of the largest of the world's wild cattle exists in the Bandhavgarh area. Built like a football linebacker, the massive jet-black body of an Indian bison, or gaur, has a muscular ridge down its back and is commanding in its strength. It weighs about 2000 pounds (900 kg) and is about 6 feet 4 inches (195 cm) tall at the shoulder. The average spread of its horns is about 33 inches (85 cm) with a huge head and big brown eyes. Amazingly, a strong adult tiger can take down an adult gaur, but it can be mortally wounded by its horns or kicking hooves while doing so. Gaurs grunt, snort, and make low bellowing sounds when they sense a tiger's presence.

A herd of wide-eyed and alert chital drink in the cool shade at Chorbehra Waterhole.

19

Indian Gazelle (*Gazella gazella*) (*Chinkara—Hindi*)

Indian gazelles have a graceful, slender body with light chestnut coloring and white on the flanks and backside. Look for the typical white streak down each side of the face. An adult male measures about 26 inches (65 cm) at the shoulder and weighs about 50 pounds (23 kg). Their S-shaped horns are about 10–12 inches long (25–30 cm) with 15 to 25 embedded ridge-like rings. They are shy, live in small herds, and usually come out to graze late in the day. They can go without water for long periods of time, deriving moisture from the plants they eat. They are easily alarmed when they sense the slightest danger.

Barking Deer (*Muntiacus muntjak*) (*kakar—Hindi*)

Muntjac, or barking deer, have short antlers—about 5 inches (13 cm) long—and a brown fur coat with dark ridges down each side of the face. They stand about 20–30 inches (50–75 cm) high and weigh about 50 pounds (23 kg). They tend to hide in thick jungle areas, graze on the edge of the forest, and make only brief visits to the waterhole. Their alarm call sounds like the bark of a dog.

Blue Bull (*Boselaphus tragocamelus*) (*nilgai—Hindi*)

The blue bull, or nilgai, is the largest Asian antelope, standing about 50–55 inches (130–140 cm) high. The adult male has a coarse gray coat and cone-like horns about 8 inches (20 cm) long. Females are tawny. Able to go without water for long periods even in hot weather, blue bulls risk fewer tiger attacks at the waterhole. They have a grunting alarm call. There are only a few blue bull herds living in the grass and scrub areas of Bandhavgarh.

Tracking a Legend

Bacchi needs to hunt frequently to keep her strength for nursing the cubs. She has fed them meat since they were about two months old. She hunts every two or three days, favoring large sambar. If the family's feeding is disrupted —by, for example, Charger—Bacchi and cubs sometimes move on, dissatisfied, and have to make another hunt.

Left: The sambar is at home in the water eating aquatic plants while a cattle egret (*Bubulcus ibis*) conveniently rests while taking aim for some nearby insects.

Right: Indian gazelles, barking deer, and blue bulls (top to bottom), as well as monkeys, sloth bears, and even villagers are all attracted to the mahua fruit, banyan tree fruit, and kumbi blossoms. Tigers have learned to hunt when their prey is distracted and preoccupied.

Indian gazelle

Barking deer

Blue bull

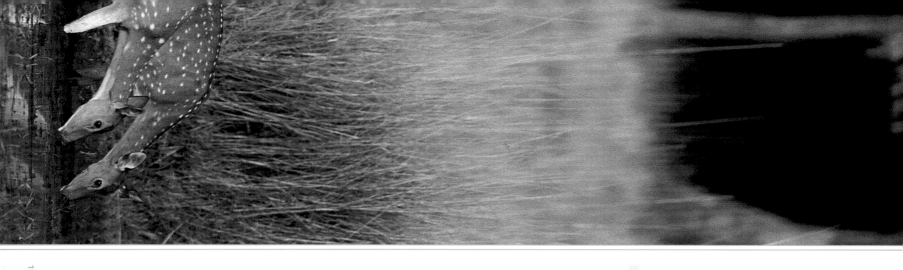

19

How can the tracker anticipate the movements of a deer herd?

During mating season, the deer's loud calls can often signal the herd's location. Check for hoof prints in streambeds and on meadow trails. Deer are irresistibly drawn to fallen blossoms and will immediately move to areas where they occur. They also eat fruit that monkeys have dropped from trees.

Above: Bachhi uses her binocular vision and sharp eyes to focus on her target in the deer herd.

Left: A chital stag stands on guard as the herd drinks at Bhadrashila Meadow's waterhole at dusk. The ultrasound frequencies a deer can hear—its hearing is equal to or perhaps even better than a tiger's—may allow it to detect the approaching predator.

ANTICIPATE DIFFERENT HUNTING TECHNIQUES

Tigers use various hunting techniques based on the situation. Sometimes they hide in bamboo thickets, tall meadow grasses, or low-lying ditches near a waterhole and patiently wait for the prey to come within easy striking distance. Other times tigers have success stalking their prey, usually deer herds. Either way, tigers—one of the world's most proficient hunters—still must make at least ten or twenty attempts for every successful hunt of their alert, alarm-call-oriented prey. When unsuccessful, a tiger may go for days without food. Check the stomach area. A hungry tiger will be lean and constantly on the hunt.

One reason for the tiger's tremendous hunting success is its forward-facing eyes with extremely accurate binocular vision. Binocular vision—like humans'—allows a tiger to quickly scan distant movements and accurately pinpoint the prey's distance. Its tremendous wide-angle vision and excellent night vision also increase its hunting advantage.

The tiger's whole body is adapted for hunting: its hind legs are longer than its forelegs, making it a powerful jumper, and it is particularly adept at grasping with its forelimbs. A tiger's front legs and shoulders are a powerhouse of muscles, and its soft footpads help it move silently. Its physical flexibility helps it navigate rough terrain with ease while hunting.

By about eleven months, tiger cubs have had enough experience observing their mother hunting and have practiced wrestling and stalking with their siblings. The tigress now introduces them to the hunt by disabling a small deer for them to catch.

The cubs learn the tiger's four-part hunting technique: scan, stalk, freeze, and seize. First, they hide silently, carefully watching their prey. Then they stalk, getting as close to the prey as possible. They freeze, and then they attack. The tiger's predatory prowess grows with daily hunting experience.

All prey is attacked differently, depending on its size and the situation. Some animals, such as small chital, are grabbed by the hindquarters and then killed by a bite to the front of the neck. Larger animals, such as sambar, are seized by the throat with a killing bite. And smaller prey—such as an Indian hare, monkey, or even peacock—are often killed by a neck-snapping bite from behind. The wild boar, with its hugely thick neck and strong damaging tusks, is a very tough challenge for the tiger. Tigers mount surprise attacks on small boars, ambushing them and then killing them with a bite to the neck. Every tiger senses the optimal hunting maneuver for each situation, based on the location and kind of prey and the camouflage opportunities provided by the terrain. They learn through experience.

Banda has fought for his territory, as the claw marks on his backside will attest. His stripes and yellow-orange body blend with the golden meadow grasses as he scans, looking for sambar, and then begins his stealthy stalking approach.

Left: Banda quietly slinks through the inner paths of the 14-foot (4 m) tall Rajbehra Meadow grasses on his soft-padded paws. He targets select sambar deer movement and freezes, using his acute depth perception to focus his attack on the prey. A tiger can run at about 35 miles per hour (56 km per hour) over a short distance, with the goal of grabbing the prey's hindquarters with its powerful claws, and then bringing it down.

Right, top: Sambar deer spies Banda on the prowl, gives a barking alarm call, and escapes.

Right, bottom: Banda, at eighteen months, gives voice to a hair-raising series of roars, and his throaty bellows are echoed by his brother Nakkatta ("Scar-Face"), calling in answer. In the process of separating from their mother, the two males cooperated, hunting together a few times before they broke away, each on his own. In the midst of this rarely photographed transition, they rest before the evening hunt.

Next page: The tiger lurks in the grassy undergrowth, hoping prey will pass his way, watching everything intensely. Stillness is the tactic. Suddenly, he snaps to attention, and his eyes dilate fully as he sights a deer limping close by.

EXPERIENCE THE TIGER'S HUNT: SCAN, STALK, FREEZE, AND SEIZE

A tiger's hunt can take minutes or hours and involves scanning for prey, silently stalking, freezing, and then attacking. Tigers, who are at their hunting prime from about three to ten years of age, are keenly intelligent and play the hunting game like a chess champion.

Scan: Keeping Pace with the Herds

Sweeping its eyes across the open meadows, an enterprising tiger can predict where the chital and large sambar are moving to graze. It looks for any irregularities of movements in the deer herd, such as a limping deer or a newborn fawn. The tiger will move in quickly if it senses an easy capture. Other times, it's a longer process—thirty minutes to an hour—involving a series of maneuvers to get close to the herd without detection.

After scanning the terrain, Banda locates a chital herd moving into the deep grasses of the Chakradhara Meadow. While they drink at the stream, they will be distracted, giving Banda the advantage. Notice the scars on his nose from territorial fights with other tigers.

Above: A solitary stalker, Banda continues the hunt for the chital by crouching low on all four feet, making slow moves toward the prey. During the hunt, Banda counts on the powerful muscles and strong bones in his legs, shoulders, and spine to help him dominate the prey with its swinging hooves and horns.

Right: Banda's low posture and laser aim builds his readiness for the attacking rush. The length and strength of a tiger's skull and its four long canine teeth (2.5 inches/6.4 cm) make it able to issue an inescapable suffocating bite to the prey's neck (a compression bite). The loss of a tiger's canines could make it incapable of hunting and bring its survival into question.

Stalk: Crouching Tigers

Above: The tiger goes into stealth mode, blending into the tall grasses and seamlessly weaving its way in a zigzag pattern in a series of slow, calculated moves. It needs to hide from its prey but also from other alarm-calling wildlife. Even a little nervous red-wattled lapwing can disrupt the hunt with its noisy alarm calls. All the tiger's senses are at their peak. The tiger is in stealth mode—totally quiet!

Freeze: The Moment Before the Attack

Right: The tiger's silent slink and fierce freeze give its eyes time to zero in on the target so it can determine the right amount of speed for capture. It approaches to within 30–60 feet (10–20 m) of its prey before the seizing rush. The tiger prepares for the unpredictable movements of the prey, hoping to trap it against water or a rocky area. The prey is in the danger zone.

Seize: Fatal Rush

Left: When the time is right, the tiger takes off like a rocket with fangs. With its yellow eyes wide open, round pupils fully dilated, and nostrils sucking in oxygen, it bursts forward in a short, powerful run. In its short sprint to catch the prey, a two-to-six-year-old in its prime has the potential to leap a distance of about 15 feet (4.5 m). It grasps and positions the deer with its large, flexible front paws and claws, presses it down with its body, and then sinks its large interlocking canine teeth into the animal's throat, suffocating it. The tiger needs to move quickly to avoid being injured by thrashing antlers and kicking hooves. The tiger's carnassials, scissor-like cutting back teeth, help it effectively eat large amounts of meat. Killing and eating prey is essential for a carnivore, yet to do so it risks potentially fatal injury. Every hunt brings life and takes life.

Predator and Possession: Eating the Prey

Right: Depending on its level of hunger, the tiger may eat right away, or it may hide the prey first and then rest. After licking the fur off the deer with its rasp-like tongue, it starts feeding from the rump and hind legs and then moves onto the abdominal organs. A tigress eats first and then shares the food with her young. A male tiger shares food with a female if they are mating. After eating, the tiger often moves to the waterhole to drink.

Left: The morning calm is shattered by the warning barks of monkey and deer as Banda explodes out of the tall grass. The blur of action ends with his massive jaws clamping onto the neck of an unlucky chital buck. He raises his head and drags the carcass away, shoulder muscles rippling, to avoid hungry swooping vultures who want his catch. His flexible spine and shoulders gave him the agility to lengthen his stride during the chase.

Above: After Banda's successful siege of the chital stag, he rests and begins swallowing large chunks of meat, eating a massive amount (40 pounds/18 kg) in one sitting. The tiger has thirty teeth. Its molars help it chew muscle, and the six incisors in the front help scrape food from the deer's leg bone.

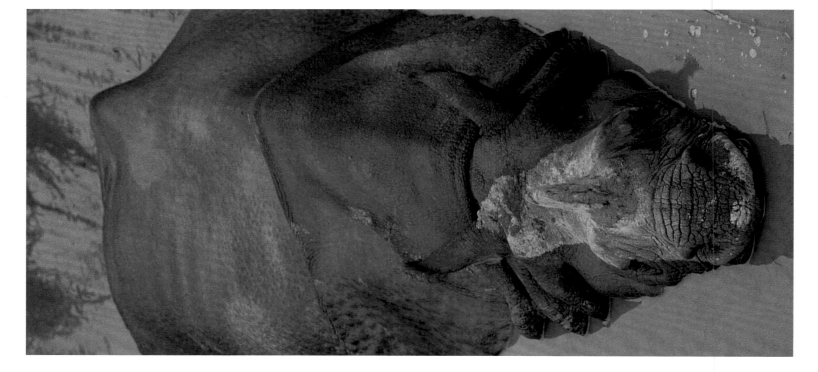

WILD TIGERS TODAY: ALIVE IN ASIA

Tigers are found in the Russian Far East, China, Indochina, India, and on the Greater Sunda Islands of Sumatra. They are remarkably adaptive, living in temperate and tropical forests, mangrove swamps, and tall grasslands. Human-tiger encounters and loss of habitat and prey are putting extreme pressure on wild tigers. As the tiger's prey disappears, so does the tiger. Three of the eight tiger subspecies (Javan, Caspian, and Bali) are extinct, and the South China tiger is moving in that direction. Siberian, Bengal, Sumatran, and Indochinese tigers are seriously endangered, and their situation will become only more desperate if poaching and destruction of habitat and prey continue.

Some 5000–7000 wild tigers remain in the world, and 3000–4500 are thought to live in India. Though these numbers are dramatically depleted—at the turn of the nineteenth century, there were 40,000 Bengal tigers in India—their current situation is considered better than that of other tiger subspecies. This is due in large part to India's Project Tiger, a massive conservation initiative started in 1973 that has established twenty-three reserves to sustain tigers, their habitat, and their wild prey. This program currently covers 12,740 square miles (33,000 sq km) in fourteen states.

Seeing a wild tiger is magic, but this experience is becoming increasingly rare. The hope for the future is in the hands of forest managers, government leaders, and local citizens as they responsibly decide to protect their lands and wildlife for the generations to come. Rediscover and make a commitment to keeping the living legend of the tiger.

Left: The Greater Indian One-horned Rhinoceros (*Rhinoceros unicornis*) (*gainda*—Hindi) is best known for its deeply folded thick skin around its neck, its prehistoric-looking armorplated body, and the single horn on its nose, which grows throughout its life and can be regrown if lost. Only about 2000 Indian rhinos remain in the wild in India. Bengal tigers and Indian rhinos coexist, though tigers will hunt young rhinos. The average Indian rhino is about 5.5 feet (1.6 m) at shoulder height and weighs about 4000 pounds (1820 kg).

Were tigers around when dinosaurs roamed the earth?

Tigers (and all other carnivores) are descended from civet-like animals called miacids that lived 60 million years ago, after the extinction of the dinosaurs. These small mammals, with long bodies and short flexible limbs, evolved over millions of years into several hundred different species, including cats, bears, dogs, and weasels. Approximately 37 cat species exist today, including *Panthera tigris*, the tiger. Tigers evolved in eastern Asia over two million years ago.

If countries with wild tigers will protect larger areas, the hope of keeping tigers free will live on.

Tiger distribution data:
Wildlife Conservation Society/
World Wildlife Fund

Map: Julie Ruff, Redstone Studios

RUSSIA

KAZAKHSTAN

MONGOLIA

CHINA

IRAN

PAKISTAN

AFGHANISTAN

TURKMENISTAN

UZBEKISTAN

TAJIKISTAN

KYRGYZSTAN

Caspian Sea

INDIA

NEPAL

BHUTAN

BANGLADESH

MYANMAR

LAOS

THAILAND

VIETNAM

CAMBODIA

SRI LANKA

Bay of Bengal

Arabian Sea

INDIAN OCEAN

SUMATRA

MALAYSIA

JAVA

BALI

INDONESIA

TAIWAN

NORTH KOREA

SOUTH KOREA

JAPAN

PACIFIC OCEAN

Where Wild Tigers Live: 2000
Where Wild Tigers Lived: 1900
Status of endangered wild tigers (2000 estimate)
Total: 5000–7000 tigers (*Panthera tigris*)
Current/Potential Habitat
Siberian (Amur): 300–400
Bengal (Indian): 3000–4500
Indo-Chinese: 1200–1700
Sumatran: 400–500
South China (Amoy): 20–30
Extinct tiger species: Bali,
Caspian, Javan

Siberian tiger

SIBERIAN, SUMATRAN, AND WHITE TIGERS

Tigers, the largest land carnivore, live only in Asia. The Siberian (or Amur) tiger (*Panthera tigris altaica*) subspecies, the biggest, lives mostly in the Russian Far East in the Sikhote-Alin Mountains. A few are found in northeastern China and northern North Korea. The forests they roam have coniferous trees, scrub oak, and birch woodlands. Only about 300–400 Siberian tigers remain in the wild.

The Siberian tiger's orange fur is the palest of all tigers', helping it blend with the white winter landscapes of the far north. Its body stripes are often brown, not black, and are the most widely spaced. Its coarse ruff of white fur around the neck is most pronounced in males.

At birth, a Siberian tiger cub weighs about 2 pounds (1000 g) and at one year is a formidable 150–200 pounds (68–90 kg). The larger a tiger's body mass including muscles and skeletal structure, the better it will be able to survive. Mature male Siberian tigers are from 8 feet 10 inches to 10 feet 10 inches (2.7–3.3 m) long from head to tail and weigh 400–675 pounds (180–306 kg). Females, 220–370 pounds (100–167 kg), are 7 feet 11 inches to 9 feet (2.4–2.75 m) in length.

Sumatran tiger

Sumatran tigers (*Panthera tigris sumatrae*), genetically distinct from all other tigers and isolated on the tropical island of Sumatra, are the smallest of all living tigers. There are only about 400–500 remaining in the wild. Their fur coat is an intense dark reddish-orange, and they have closely spaced black stripes on their body and forelegs. An average male Sumatran tiger ranges from 7 to 8 feet (2–2.4 m) in length and weighs be-

tween 220 and 310 pounds (100–140 kg). The home range of a Sumatran tiger in a rainforest area with good prey is about 39 square miles (100 sq km), supporting three or four tigers.

Are saber-tooth tigers (Smilodon) related to other tigers?

They are not ancestors of today's tigers and belong to a separate branch of cat family that became extinct 11,000 years ago.

20+

143

Tiger Mating

White tigers are not true albinos (which lack dark skin pigment), and their eyes are blue, not pink. As with all tigers the pattern of striping–in the case of white tigers, the stripes are gray, brown, and black–and the facial patterns give each white tiger its unique look.

White tigers are born from yellow-orange tigers that carry a rare white recessive gene. They are born in litters with normal yellow-orange tigers. If each tiger parent has the recessive gene, at least one of the four cubs is likely to have white fur. Inbreeding among captive tigers with the recessive gene does weaken the health of white tigers and creates controversy in the practices of tiger conservation.

The higher the latitude where they live—the colder the environment—the bigger the tiger. The largest Siberian tiger ever recorded weighed about 1025 pounds (465 kg)—a goliath predator. Siberians have thick, shaggy fur, which grows to about 4 inches (105 mm) in length, making it possible for them to tolerate extreme winter cold, down to -31° F (-35° C). By comparison, the fur of the Bengal tiger, which lives in a warm climate, is only about 1.35 inches (35 mm) long.

Siberians' territories are large, due to the low density of their prey—elk, red deer, roe deer, sika deer, and wild boar. A female's home range can be 39–154 square miles (100–400 sq km) and a male's is 309–390 square miles (800–1000 sq km). The more prey, the smaller territories become, and more tigers can fit into the habitat. Adaptive and resilient to changing conditions, tigers survive. To monitor their numbers, scientists check the tracks these wild tigers leave in the snow, which helps them assess the success of their conservation initiatives.

Dangerous Liaison
A male white Siberian tiger holds the female with a gripping bite during mating. She is a yellow-orange Siberian. Since both have the recessive gene, this mating could produce white tigers.

Left: Two-month-old Siberian tiger cub climbing a rock.

Right: Newborns, with their eyes still closed. They are unable to see for about the first two weeks of life.

20+

Tiger Litter

Newborn Siberian tiger cubs weigh about 2 pounds (1000 g) but grow up fast. By one year they are a formidable 150–200 pounds (68–90 kg). The race to grow and gain strength to succeed in their challenging environment is lost by about 50 percent of tiger cubs, who do not make it past the first six months of life.

20+

Bengal white tiger

Tiger Litter

Mohan, the father of all white tigers, was discovered in 1951 as a nine-month-old cub near what is now the Bandhavgarh Tiger Reserve. By breeding Mohan to his daughter Mohini, the white tiger's genes were carried forward to the roughly 200 captive white tigers in the world today. Wild white tigers were recorded in India as early as the sixteenth century, but none are known to exist in the wild today. The white tigers pictured here (Siberian and Bengal) are distant relatives of Mohan. Look into their blue eyes.

Siberian white tiger

20 WAYS TO SAVE WILD TIGERS

Tigers are one of the world's natural treasures, and they are seriously endangered. What can you do to help save them, their lands, and their prey? Some situations can be improved through a combination of global and local partnerships. Refer to the list of websites below and use your personal and professional networks and resources to make a difference. Stay informed by finding your favorite tiger websites and checking them often. Take action on some of the items listed below. Tigers' survival depends on us.

1. Stop the Tiger Trade

Never buy or possess products that claim to contain tiger bone. (These can be found in certain Asian communities.) Not only are they illegal, but they rarely contain tiger and perpetuate the myth that tiger parts can cure disease. Be a keen observer and confidentially report illegal tiger trading activities to local authorities, consulates, or television stations around the world. By helping sway public opinion, the media can create the pressure to stop the tiger trade. Review the *www.worldwildelife.org* Buyer Beware site.

2. Prosecute Wildlife Criminals (Poachers and Buyers)

The annual global illegal wildlife trade is estimated to be about $25 billion and is now the second largest illegal occupation in the world. Implement and enforce wildlife-protection laws swiftly to set a serious standard to prevent extinctions. A tiger can be killed by eating a poisoned deer left by a waterhole; poachers make a quick getaway without ever firing a shot. The Wildlife Protection Society of India (www.wpsi-india.org) actively identifies and prosecutes wildlife criminals.

3. Buy Trees for Tigers

Fewer than 350 adult Siberian tigers survive in the forests of the Russian Far East. Loss of habitat and prey have contributed to the crisis. Avoid buying hardwood timber from the Asian wilderness. The nonprofit conservation organization American Forests is helping to expand tiger habitat in

Russia by working with local villagers and scientists to plant Korean pine trees that provide cover along corridors that connect protected tiger reserves. The pine nuts are eaten by the native deer and wild boar, which are the prey of the Siberian tiger. Form a Trees for Tigers team in your school or community to raise money for buying trees. To plant Trees for Tigers for $1 each (and get a free Trees for Tigers T-shirt by planting 35 trees or more), call 800/545-TREE (8733) or visit *www.treesfortigers.org*.

4. Help Local People Preserve the Forest

Prevent forest fires near villages and in tiger reserves by training and equipping local villagers. Also, provide financial incentives to encourage the local residents to use fuel-efficient stoves and solar cookers. Foraging in the forest area puts people and tigers at risk.

5. Give Generously to Proactive Tiger Conservation Organizations

Visit tiger conservation websites and review their local initiatives to protect tigers and help villagers. Target your donations to specific tiger field projects that mean the most to you. Have your organization sponsor a specific tiger conservation initiative. Use VISA cards through banks that donate money to major wildlife conservation organizations. Add your favorite wildlife conservation group to your will.

6. Expand Tiger Reserves

Buy and protect tiger habitat in India and throughout Asia so tigers can roam freely when searching for prey. Extend select existing tiger reserves and create new protected areas to help growing tiger populations in unprotected lands. Work closely with villagers throughout any relocation to ensure they are compensated and included in the change process. In India, only about half the wild tigers live in or near tiger reserves, leaving the other half at greater risk of fatal human-tiger conflicts. Check the Project Tiger site (http://envfor.nic.in/pt/) for an understanding of tiger reserve land needs.

This golden Siberian tiger cub is a color variation whose origins lie in the recessive gene of the white tiger. The skull is from a member of its family.

Status of endangered wild tigers (2003 estimates)

Total: 5,000–7,000 tigers
Amur (Siberian): 300–400
Bengal (Indian): 3000–4500
Indo-Chinese: 1200–1700
South China (Amoy): 20–30
Sumatran: 400–500
Extinct tiger species: Bali, Caspian, Javan

7. Support Local Wildlife Conservation Education

Educate local villagers to be good tiger neighbors. Support wildlife conservation organizations that work to educate villagers to avoid taking tiger prey. Help villagers locate other food sources, meaning that tigers will be less likely to roam beyond their home range. Also teach them to tolerate situations in which a tiger might take some of their cattle. Promote nature education to the local community with sponsored visits to the tiger reserves to build an understanding of tigers.

8. Care for Families of Tiger Attack Victims

Support the families of individuals attacked by tigers who live near tiger reserves. Ensure they are cared for with support from forest officials and the community.

9. Stop Use of High-Voltage Electrified Fences

Farmers with lands bordering tiger reserves are using electrified fences in increasing numbers. Fund a local community program to stop farmers from rigging their fences to administer high-voltage shocks, which can instantly kill roaming prey and tigers as well.

10. Fund, Train, and Reward Tiger Anti-Poaching Patrols

Train anti-poaching patrols with upgraded equipment, and offer rewards for capture of poachers. Seize all weapons and deal severely with the poachers. Fund nighttime tiger jeep patrols, especially during monsoon season when few people are around. Poachers often enter a tiger reserve at night and go to where they know the tiger is frequently seen.

11. Promote Good Relationships Between Forest Officials and Villagers

Reward local forest officials for engaging, influencing, and training local villagers in the protection of tiger habitats. Help officials enforce illegal cutting of trees and grasses that are needed to sustain the tiger's prey.

12. Support the Science of Tiger Conservation

Develop more scientific information about the biodiversity of the tiger reserve areas to help win further support for conservation. Learn more about the tiger population density in a location. (Contact www.wcs.org.)

13. Engage the Government in Policies, Practices, and Funding to Support Tiger Conservation

Gain national government support and international funding to support existing and new tiger conservation initiatives. Start a campaign among your friends to write or call key politicians and national wildlife directors who fund tiger conservation programs.

14. Ensure that Local Villagers Profit from Ecotourism

Promote responsible tiger tourism and encourage local people and travelers to witness the tiger in the wild. This unforgettable experience will make many people new friends of the tiger. Be sure that villagers benefit from local ecotourism. For instance, villagers could buy a jeep to use for tourism, develop their abilities as forest guides, and gain steady employment.

15. Do Good Things for the Community in the Name of the Tiger

Partner with NGOs to help the local community with their health and well-being, letting them know the program is sponsored by a tiger initiative.

16. Recognize the Champions of Tiger Conservation

Offer programs providing a certificate of special achievement and financial rewards to forest officials who specialize in tigers and forest management to help restore the tiger's habitat and deforestation due to human destruction.

17. Support Global and Local Politicians Who Enforce Tiger Conservation Laws

Support proactive politicians who support strong international conservation laws such as the Endangered Species Act and the Rhino and Tiger Conservation Act. Review updates on the Convention on International Trade of Endangered Species at www.cites.org.

18. Focus the Media on Positive Actions to Address the Tiger's Crisis

Keep the media's attention on tiger conservation by creating public service announcements and focus the public's ability to influence change in favor of the tiger and its habitat. Request current films and media stories on tigers for prime-time programming.

19. *Special ways to learn more about wild tigers*

• Watch the *Tigers—Tracking a Legend* film/DVD with family, friends, and colleagues. Discuss the story, fun tiger facts, and how to help save endangered wild tigers today.

• Draw pictures of tigers before watching the DVD, and then draw more pictures afterwards. Discuss the similarities and differences between the tiger drawings.

• Have fun taking the tiger quiz on the *Tigers—Tracking a Legend* DVD.

• Look at the photographs in this book and describe to others the tiger's life and habitat. Lend the book to your friends.

• Encourage kids of all ages to draw pictures of wild tigers and their habitat and describe special aspects (tiger families, special tiger body features, tiger predator-prey relationships, human-tiger relationships, etc.) to each other.

• Write a song or poem about wild tigers and share it with others.

• Devote a public display area to tiger drawings, poems, and discussions.

• Organize a dedicated tiger science project in school on tiger evolution, DNA testing, and genetics.

• Find Siberia, India, and Sumatra on a map and identify where wild tigers live. Learn about the culture of the local people, and discover ways to save wild tigers and their habitats.

20. *Save wild tigers by supporting dedicated and experienced organizations that communicate with local people and do the science to understand the tiger in its unique environment.*

Wildlife Conservation Society   *wcs.org*
Visit WCS's Tiger Mountain, the Bronx Zoo's spectacular, three-acre interactive tiger exhibit that links zoo visitors with field conservation efforts.

The Tiger Information Center   *5tigers.org*
(Save The Tiger Fund)

The Tiger Foundation   *tigers.ca*

The Sumatran Tiger Trust   *tigertrust.info*

World Wildlife Fund   *worldwildlife.org*

Wildlife Protection Society of India   *wpsi-india.org*

The Wildlife Trust of India   *wildlifetrustofindia.org*

Tiger Territory   *lairweb.org.nz/tiger*

World Conservation Union   *iucn.org*
(Cat Specialist Group)

21st Century Tiger   *www.zsl.org*

Tigers in Crisis   *tigersincrisis.com*

American Forests   *www.treesfortigers.org*

Wildlife Worlds' Media Fund   *wildlifeworlds.com*
The mission of Wildlife Worlds' Media Fund is to secure funding to make meaningful and entertaining nature films for worldwide audiences in partnership with broadcast networks, digital cinema enterprises, and websites. Each award-winning film, like *Tigers—Tracking a Legend*, promotes the awareness of endangered wildlife issues through compelling storytelling sensitive to the interrelationship between people and animals.

A CONVERSATION WITH FILMMAKER, PHOTOGRAPHER, AND AUTHOR, CAROL AMORE

What is a day in the life of a tiger filmmaker like?

Awakened from dreaming about tigers, I'd get up at 4:15 AM to stretch (my muscles would ache from lifting heavy equipment), check my equipment, eat breakfast, and prepare for the day. At 5:00 the jeep would bring two of us and our equipment into the reserve, and tracking would begin as we looked for tiger paw prints in the dirt road. Soon we'd meet up with mahavats and head out on the elephants through the dense forest with no roads, checking waterholes or the areas where tigers were last seen. We'd be back by about 10–11:00 AM, dehydrated and exhausted from the sweltering 110° F/43° C heat. At 3:30 we'd head out again, after having consulted forest officials, learned of the tigers' movements, and checked all video equipment, and we'd continue till the last light of dusk. After dark was the time to meet with the forest guides to discuss the afternoon's sightings and plan for the next day's filming. For fun, we'd count the number of bruises we acquired every day. At dinner, we'd screen all the video and discuss everything, ranging from technical challenges to an intense evaluation of how the images captured the spirit and the stories of the Indian jungle, its wildlife, and the intimate behaviors of the Bengal tigers.

What was the toughest part of filming tigers?

Finding the tigers. You have to use a sixth sense and everyone's jungle intuition to read the signs and sounds of the jungle that lead to locating a tiger within its territory. Some days we found no tigers, but sometimes we were able to film the mother and cubs eating, relaxing, and even playing—a good day. I often filmed from atop a heavy custom-designed 10-foot tripod with a rotating seat. Maneuvering from an elephant's back onto the tripod was risky; it was hard to position it firmly on uneven surfaces in rough terrain. During filming sometimes a cub would frolic over and start to try to climb the tripod with the tigress closely watching. One slip, and the camera and cameraperson would fall to the hard, rocky ground. We knew the risks, however, and were committed to continue.

Were you ever afraid?

Fear in the jungle can be fatal. Thinking quickly and knowing the jungle and its wildlife can help protect an animal and save your life at the same time. I will say, though, that it's hard to stay quiet when a poisonous krait snake is coming into the film hide and there is a tigress who is highly protective of her cubs outside at the waterhole. One night a leopard killed a deer outside my window with a wrestle, a struggle, a thud, and then silence. The leopard's frequent night visits made me highly alert, always looking for its silhouette in the trees or on the ground. Another time a pack of feral dogs moved in on me while I was walk-

Carol photographed tigers from inside this *machan*, a bamboo and grass hide, which allowed her to be on the edge of the Thaudi Waterhole without being noticed by the wildlife. Total silence was needed and food, which could attract animals, was forbidden. Snakes moving through the *machan* would occasionally disrupt filming.

Left: Carol editing slides in her New York City photo gallery.
Photo: Arnold Newman

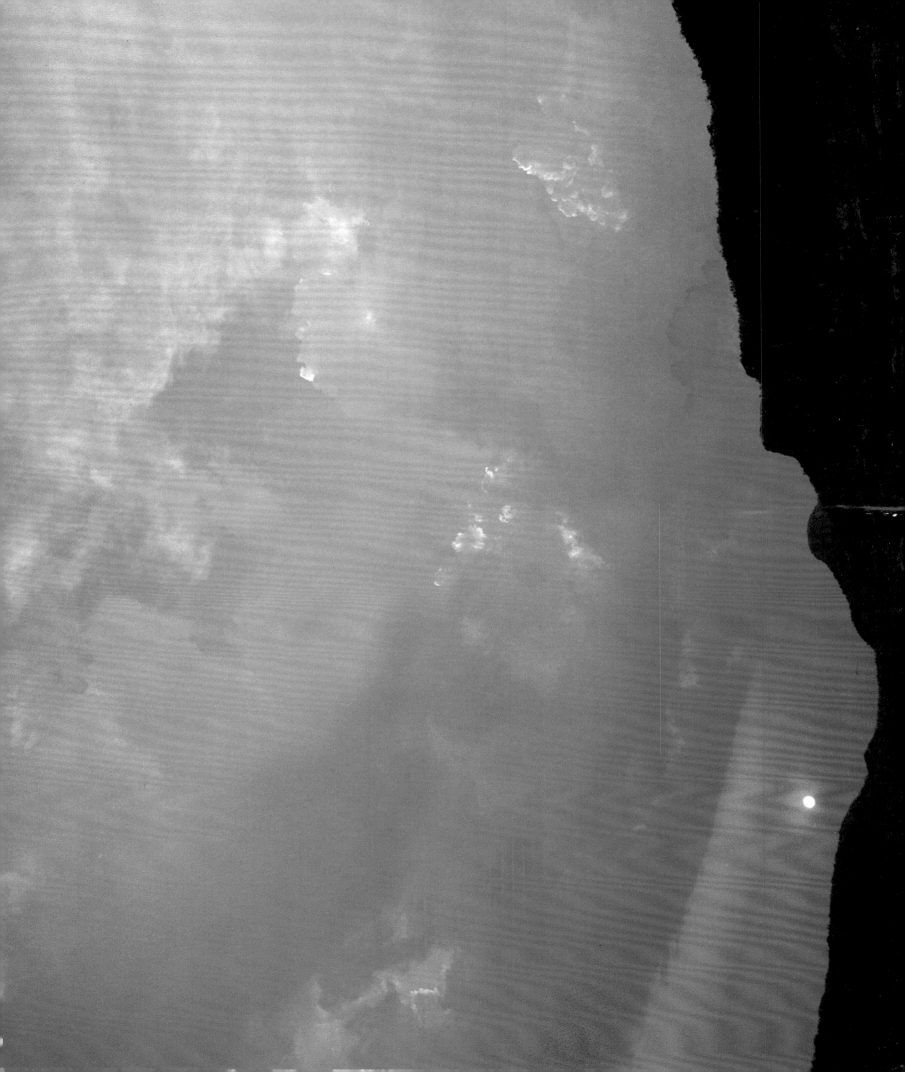